How to Use The Heart of Youth Ministry

The principles in this book can be used to develop a youth ministry from the ground up. It doesn't matter if you have a group of six, sixty or six hundred. That's because the plan doesn't involve a complicated program. Instead, this revolutionary concept of ministry is based on building relationships with teens.

The strategies outlined in *The Heart of Youth Ministry* will help you learn to reach young people no matter what their stage of spiritual development because you will use four distinct levels of ministry:

1. Come level—drawing in non-Christians or minimally committed Christians through non-threatening activities.

2. Grow level—helping youth grow in their commitments to Christ and helping them develop Christian disciplines such as prayer and Bible study.

3. Discipleship level—teaching young people to apply scriptural principles to their daily lives.

4. Leadership level—training youth to be disciplers of others.

You will also learn some valuable principles about strengthening your own relationship with God. And you will gain some practical insight about maintaining strong family relationships in the middle of the sometimes unpredictable world of youth.

The Heart of Youth Ministry

Building a Dynamic
Youth Ministry from the
Ground Up

The Heart of Youth Ministry

Building a Dynamic Youth Ministry from the Ground Up

By Hule Goddard and
Jorge Acevedo

BRISTOL
BOOKS
WILMORE, KY 40390

THE HEART OF YOUTH MINISTRY
Building A Dynamic Youth Ministry From The Ground Up
Copyright ©1989 by Hule Goddard and Jorge Acevedo
Published by Bristol Books

First Edition, January 1989

Library of Congress Card Number:88-72132
ISBN:0-917851-15-3
Suggested Subject Headings:
1.Group Ministry
2.Church Work With Youth
Recommended Dewey Decimal Classification:259.23

BRISTOL BOOKS
An imprint of Good News, a Forum for Scriptural Christianity, Inc.
308 East Main Street • Wilmore, Kentucky 40390

For Loretta and Cheryl, our loving wives

Contents

Foreword

It was in 1983 that I began to sense God leading me into a new role of teaching youth ministry at Eastern College in St. Davids, Pennsylvania. It was a challenge that brought with it a wealth of questions, doubts and concerns. Not the least of which was what would happen to the youth program I was leaving behind at the Wilmore United Methodist Church in Wilmore, Kentucky.

Admittedly, my biggest concern was how and whether the church would choose to fill my soon to be vacant position. Right in the middle of this process of looking ahead to the new position and looking back to some great years of ministry, I made it my personal responsibility to also look around for a replacement. It was in that search that I first made contact with a young youth minister from Texas named Hule Goddard.

I had heard good reports about Hule's work, but I still had questions. I can't really adequately justify the kind of skepticism that floods your mind when you are choosing your own successor. I suppose it's like choosing a husband for your youngest daughter. Nobody seems good enough. All kinds of questions are raised. Will he know how to handle this one? Will he give those enough attention? Will he understand the uniqueness of this community? Will he respect the traditions and directions that have preceded him? Will the church be able to accept a youth minister with a full head of hair? Is it fair to ask a church to go from having a youth minister named "Duffy" to a youth minister named "Hule"?

But those days are now a half a decade behind us, and the worries and fears of those days are long gone. My ministry here at Eastern College has been beyond anything I might have imagined. And, the youth group at the Wilmore United Methodist Church has surpassed any goals and dreams I had ever dared to put in a written report. The youth program's outreach to fringe kids has increased dramatically, and the ongoing ministries of equipping and discipling have been further sharpened and refined by Hule Goddard and his team of volunteers.

Now, when I go back to Wilmore, the people at the UM Church say, "Duffy who?"

I know why God has blessed this ministry so much over the last few years under Hule's direction. The answer is simple: This is a ministry with heart. It's a ministry with passion! For most teenagers today, the ideas of passion and God are almost never connected. Passion is something you see on afternoon television shows that feature characters with names like Roman and Marlena.

But that is beginning to change. Hard as it is to believe, I know some kids who now, when they think of passion, think of a loving God, and a youth minister named Hule.

And that's what this book is about. It's a book that doesn't so much teach as it bleeds. We are reading words here that pulse with the very heartbeat of two of the country's finest youth ministers, Hule Goddard and Jorge Acevedo. This is a book that you don't read simply for education. You read it for "transfusion."

Don't get me wrong. The concepts are here. Jorge Acevedo and Hule Goddard are accomplished professionals who know their stuff. They both have track records of effective ministry with teenagers, and they are widely respected among those who know of their work. But this is not a dry treatise that brings us some new "ministry model." This is a fresh and heartfelt plea for a vision and ministry style.

What we have in *The Heart of Youth Ministry* is nothing less than a manifesto from two youth ministers who share with us their passion and their commitment to relational youth ministry. As much as this notion of relational ministry is talked about, it's high time that we were given some practical, step-by-step advice on how to translate this passion into a way of doing daily ministry. That, I think, is the strength of this book. It gives us more than "heart," it gives us "head," "hands" and "feet." It tells us how.

In the years since I left Wilmore, I've had a chance to see a lot of youth programs and meet a lot of youth ministers. But, I will always be grateful to God that he allowed me to rub elbows with people of passion and vision like Hule Goddard and Jorge Acevedo. These guys are building a future for the United Methodist Church—not by building new buildings or raising big dollars, but by building disciples and raising up teenagers who have a vision and love for God.

Sometimes, in my travels, people ask me why I still feel hopeful about the United Methodist Church. Well, you, the reader, are holding in your hands one of the number one reasons. It's not because of some new conference or appointment or biennial emphasis. It's because God is raising up within this denomination some people who are more interested in fulfilling a commission than sitting on one. And to that I say, "Praise the Lord."

My prayer is that as you read this book, God will begin to quicken your pulse with a love for him, and a love for the teenagers in your community with whom he wants desperately to begin a life-long relationship. Because in the end, that's where strong youth ministry begins. I think Jorge Acevedo and Hule Goddard understand that. I know they demonstrate it. At "the heart of youth ministry" is a heart for God and his people. The passion and the practice are what this book is all about.

Duffy A. Robbins, Eastern College,
St. Davids PA.

CHAPTER 1

The Heart of Youth Ministry

The Results of a Relational, Discipleship-oriented Ministry with Youth

By Hule Goddard

Jay was a quiet, well-liked, brilliant young man growing up in New Albany, Mississippi. But although those who knew him thought he showed promise, no one guessed that one day he would exert a world-changing influence for Christ.

Bo Moffat, the youth Sunday school teacher at the local Methodist church, took an interest in Jay. In time, this relationship helped Jay make a solid, life-long commitment to Christ. In the years that followed, Jay, Mr. Moffat and the youth minister spent many rich hours in conversation, laughter and prayer. God gradually fanned the spark of this young man's commitment into a force that directed his entire life.

Jay's growth was the product of a revolutionary concept of youth ministry. Unlike most highly structured youth ministries, the emphasis was on Jay himself, not on finding ways to get Jay to follow the program. But let's hear Jay tell the story.

It was hard to make myself get up and go to Mr. Moffat's Sunday school class that first morning; in fact, I'm not sure why I went. Maybe I went because it was "promotion Sunday," and I was to move to a new class of eleventh and twelfth graders. With school starting for the fall and the first football game just around the corner, my mind was a long way from church. I was a junior and had just become first chair trumpet player in the band—my greatest love.

Maybe I went to Sunday school that morning because of tradition. I had "grown up" in the church. My parents were active members and took me every Sunday until I was about twelve or thirteen. I had accepted Jesus Christ as my Savior when I was eleven, and I knew that he had given me the free gift of eternal life by dying on the cross for my sins.

But eternity seemed very far off that morning—much further than my first football game. I considered salvation something you did once and then tucked away until you died and needed to use it.

Sunday school had been fun when I was a kid, with games, songs, arts and crafts. But as I entered the junior high years, it seemed pointless to sit and half-listen to the lessons. It became merely a time to catch up with friends on who did what Saturday night. I became disillusioned, lazy and quit going.

I also dropped out of choir and youth activity, partly because I became disenchanted and because I didn't feel like I fit into the social scene very well at that age. Some of my friends would comment about my not coming to Sunday school or choir and would invite me. But I sort of resented their overtures, even though a part of me knew something was missing.

So some people were surprised to see me walk into Mr. Moffat's class that morning—it had been a long time since I'd been to church. Mr. Moffat came in a little late, with a cup of coffee in one hand and some books under his arm. He didn't spend a lot of time on introductions or asking us what we wanted to study as so many other teachers had—searching, it seemed, for something to hold the attention of a bunch of teenagers. Instead, Mr. Moffat just smiled and said that the class was "in Colossians" and would pick up where it had stopped the previous Sunday.

Copies of The Living Bible were passed out, and he

told us to open "the Word." That was an expression I had never heard before, as were many others he used. He called the Bible "God's Word" or "the Word of God," and he told us repeatedly that we had to be "in the Word" daily. He talked with a gleam in his eye about getting up early in the morning and sitting alone on his patio reading the Word.

When Mr. Moffat prayed in class it was as if Jesus were right there in the room. When Mr. Moffat talked to God, he expected to be heard "through the blood of Christ." He talked about "walking in faith," "being filled with the Spirit" and "staying prayed up." There was something about the way he talked about faith; I could tell it was vital and true-to-life for him. As he read and had us read from the Bible, he followed no lesson plan or commentary. Instead, he shared personal applications and favorite verses and described struggles in his own life. I learned that Jesus was not only my Savior but the Lord of my life.

Mr. Moffat said we should pray about our future—whether God wanted us to go to college, what career he wanted for us, even whom he wanted us to marry! He said God had a special plan for each of of us, "his will for our lives," and that we needed to seek him and fit into that will, making Jesus truly Lord of our lives.

So much of this I had never heard—or maybe I had heard it, but it had never mattered to me. This man, however, made it seem vital, as important as life itself, and as much a part of life as breathing. He challenged us to don our armor (Ephesians 6:11-17) every morning before getting out of bed, to read a chapter of Proverbs for each day of the month, to pray and study God's Word daily and to memorize Scripture (he had us begin with John 1:1).

Something about Mr. Moffat's sincerity and naturalness attracted me—his lifestyle revealed a new world to me, but I liked it. I began attending his class every Sunday and started hanging around for church services. My older sister gave me a copy of The Living Bible that Christmas of 1975, and I read through it.

I didn't become an angel; outwardly, I didn't change

much at all at first. But God was working on my heart. I committed my life to Christ and asked him to be my Lord and guide. I prayed about college and later went there with the foundation of having spent two years in Mr. Moffat's class. Leaving his class was a sad part of graduating from high school.

Another part of high school graduation was the parties. One of these was an informal get-together for the seniors at the house where the youth director, Hule Goddard, rented a room. I had heard of him—he had spent the past couple of summers as youth director at our church when he was on break from college. Our small church had always had "summer youth workers"; in fact, my big sister had been one. However, I had never been active in the youth group, not even after I became involved in Mr. Moffat's class. Being a loyal senior, though, I went to the party.

Hule seemed genuine, down-to-earth and took a personal interest in everyone right where they were in life. He even found things I was interested in to talk to me about! I heard some of the phrases Mr. Moffat used here and there in his casual conversation—"the Lord," "God's Word," "his plan," "his will." Jesus Christ was real to this youth director too!

He invited me to a weeknight youth Bible study, and for the first time, I went . . . and kept going. In fact, I hung around the church in my spare time that summer and visited with the youth director. He kidded a lot and called me "Jaybird," which I liked. We talked a lot about life in general. He let me drive the church van, and I even lead the Bible study one night. I had grown up with all the people in that youth group, but that summer I felt closer to them and more accepted by them than ever before.

The summer ended, and we all went our separate ways to college, including Hule. One of the guys who was commuting to junior college continued the weeknight Bible study for the high school folks. Hule made sure that a couple of us who went to a particular college got together for a weekly Bible study with his brother who also went there.

As I went to a new place and met new people, I was confident that God had led me in my decision to attend that school and major in pre-medicine. God continued to work in my life to provide Christian fellowship and growth opportunities, friends, roommates, courses, professors, grades and other steps along the way. I continued to "stay in the Word," as my old Sunday school teacher would say.

Mr. Moffat moved to Oklahoma, and I saw him only occasionally. The youth director finished college and came back to my home church for several years. I spent the summer after my sophomore year at home working as a hospital orderly and got to be one of the "elders" of the youth group. I have many great memories of this time—whitewater rafting trips, games of pool, campfires and the afternoon they tried to teach me to water ski. Most of all, I found encouragement to remain deeply committed to God.

I continued to play trumpet in the college band and through it met some people in a Christian music ensemble. I played trumpet with them my last two years of college, traveling to churches on weekends, going on mission trips during spring breaks, sharing what God was doing in my life and what Jesus meant to me.

As God led me to finish college, with honors, I prayed much about a career in medicine. God provided a way for me to attend a first-rate medical school on a full fellowship program that would lead to a Ph.D. degree as well as an M.D. The phone call telling me that I had been accepted came during the Christmas holidays of 1980. I remembered Mr. Moffat quoting Ephesians 3:20: "Now to him who is able to do immeasurably more than all we ask or imagine, according to his power that is at work within us, to him be glory. . . ." I thanked God for more than answering all the prayers about my future and my career.

God faithfully provided in so many ways as I went to a strange new city to attend med school. Not only did he give me strength to pass the heavy course load, but he taught me what he wanted me to know about medicine and life and more about his Son. A small

17

group on campus met for weekly Bible study and prayer. The group's number grew larger than the room could hold as more and more Christians seemed to be accepted to that med school during the next couple of years.

Then there was Blaine, a guy in my class who was also a committed Christian and had a similar story of how God had led him to med school after years of prayer. Blaine and I shared many a late night of studying, praying over tests and offering prayers of joy as God led us into dating relationships that we knew were extra special.

I could write volumes on the miracles God worked as Kathy and I dated and eventually married in February 1984. On our wedding day I remembered Mr. Moffat's admonishment to "pray about the person whom God would have you marry," and I thanked God for answering those many years of prayer. Kathy is also a committed Christian and had prayed for years for her "husband to be." God has remained faithful as he has led us through good times and bad, triumph and crisis, sleepless nights and illnesses. He has provided for us financially, physically, spiritually, emotionally and in many ways that we can realize only now as we look back at how he guided us every step of the way. He has picked us up when we have fallen and has been the strength in our weakness.

By his grace, I graduated with an M.D. and Ph.D. with honors, won national awards for my research and am now in my second year of residency training as a doctor. God has given Kathy a ministry in which she influences the lives of hundreds of college students through teaching marriage and family-living courses. We don't know exactly what God has planned for us in the future, but we know he will lead us if we continue to seek his way.

As I sit in my den this rainy Friday night, I thank God for Bo Moffat, Hule Goddard, Blaine Bishop, Kathy and so many others who have been and are gracious ministers to me.

The Sunday school teacher and youth director were following the pattern established by the apostle Paul, who tells how he drew back the curtain of his heart for ministry:

> As apostles of Christ we could have been a burden to you, but we were gentle among you, like a mother caring for her little children. We loved you so much that we were delighted to share with you not only the gospel of God but our lives as well, because you had become so dear to us (1 Thessalonians 2:7-8).

The heart of Paul's ministry, and of any successful youth ministry, is the relational dynamic described in this passage. The minister, whether youth counselor or Sunday school teacher, must go beyond building an excellent program, even beyond offering effective preaching and teaching, to actually enter the lives of those in his or her charge. By building relationships with young people, the youth worker can offer powerful, individualized ministry.

Paula knows the impact this kind of youth ministry can have. As a teenager, Paula took advantage of the opportunities available to her in her church's solid youth program, coupled with lively relational ministry. Here is Paula's testimony.

> I always received strong spiritual and biblical training at home. I accepted Jesus at a very early age; I rededicated my life and joined the United Methodist Church at age nine. My first three years in the youth group were a time of spiritual growth. The firm foundation of my Christian walk was laid, but it was not until my last three years of high school that the style of the building above the foundation was created and cemented. Each day finishing touches are added, and by God's grace the building will be an unshakable skyscraper, ever reaching up for him. (I have learned that I can never let my guard down, for Satan has a demolition team!)
>
> In late summer of one of those years in the youth group, I met a couple that God chose to influence my life. A long-time friend and I were walking out of the

church office when we were introduced to a "Grizzly Adams" type man and his wife who were to be the new youth leaders. I had a few doubts. He was a hunting and fishing man from the deep South, and he was called "Hule" (pronounced Hoo-lee). I was raised in the big city and did not even enjoy girl scouts! How could I relate to someone like him? There must have been a mistake in the hiring process, I thought.

I am convinced God has a sense of humor. He sends people across my path from whom I differ from greatly. Much to my surprise, my new youth director was someone I came to respect. God used him tremendously because he was a real person who had "no deceit"— the first to admit a fault, the first to apologize. Jesus was written all over his face. He was "a good old boy" who loved Jesus. He reached out and became a part of our world, and we became a part of his. He was definitely our leader but he was someone to count on, a friend who could meet any person on any level, rich or poor, well-liked or rejected. That is the way Jesus would have done it.

Soon after Hule and his wife came to my church, some of us were interested in pursuing deeper spiritual matters. We gathered in his office weekly for Bible study. We read about the great men and women in the Scriptures, their weaknesses and strengths. We discovered the characteristics in those leaders that we, as youth, could apply to our own lives to become outstanding men and women of God. I still periodically review Abraham, David, Ruth and Mary and look for ways I can have the same inner strength and beauty that God approved of in their lives.

In the spring, two of my girlfriends and I led an eighth grade girls' Bible study at Hule's request. What a challenge! We prayed together. We were models for them. I still remember an object lesson we taught them about peer pressure.

One of us stood on a chair (representing the Christian), and one on the floor (representing the non-Christian). We demonstrated how difficult it is to pull up a wayward friend; how much easier it is for the "bad company" to bring down the struggling Christian. I believe it helped them to better understand the problem with peers who do not support one's Christian commitment. I have always remembered that illustration when choosing friends.

My senior year in high school was the most special time that I spent in the youth group. Seven of us formed a core group that was accountable to one another. We met early for prayer, memorized Scripture, had daily devotions and planned youth activities. We were truly serious about the Lord. A few days before Thanksgiving, our group went to another Christian high school where we spent the day performing skits and sharing about Jesus in our lives. We related how Jesus can give us strength to remain true in difficult situations. My topic was purity. I have done my best to hold on to the words God gave me for those students.

I was also in charge of our youth visitation program, with Hule's guidance. I did a good job, and it built my self-esteem as I proved my leadership abilities. The Lord used me in this program to increase the number of youth visiting other youth, putting feet to our words of love.

During this time, there were choir tours to California, Mississippi and Florida, allowing countless opportunities to minister. These types of activities pushed my faith further. I not only sat in a Sunday school class and heard God's Word, but Hule also gave me places to minister and positions from which to lead. I was handed the ball and had to run with it. It was my responsibility to lead other youth; I became active for Jesus, not passive. The youth director and youth worked as a team for Jesus.

After one of my last Sunday nights in the youth group before leaving for college, I came home, stood in my bathroom and cried. I did not want to give up my wonderful youth group, friends and security. Then the Lord flashed before me all of the marvelous Christian opportunities I'd had so far. I was thankful, so thankful. In the midst of my joy, he issued a mandate from Scripture: "From everyone who has been given much,

much will be demanded" (Luke 12:48). Suddenly, I became serious. God did not give me all of that training so I could say how great I was or how wonderful my life had been, but so that I could use it.

In college I was a Christian witness. I held fast to my values. I would remind myself that God, my parents and Hule, among others, were counting on me to carry a victorious Christian banner. I had some difficult times my third year in college—hospitalized for two surgeries in eighteen months and a hurtful breakup with a boyfriend. I went through a real spiritual desert for at least a year, but God did not give up on me nor I on him. He gave me a Bible verse during those troubled times.

"Fear not, for I have redeemed you; I have called you by name; you are mine. When you pass through the waters, I will be with you; and when you pass through the rivers, they will not sweep over you. When you walk through the fire, you will not be burned; the flames will not set you ablaze. For I am the Lord, your God . . ." (Isaiah 43:1-3).

I had been trained as a Christian; I had come too far to turn back.

I graduated from Oral Roberts University in May 1987. I presently work in a secular business environment, but I am still a light in a dark world. Thank the Lord that my old friends can refer to me as "the same old Paula." All of my peers and co-workers are able to see that my conduct is different from the standard of the world.

Because I became so rooted and grounded in Christ, it would destroy me completely to remove Christ from my life. Jesus Christ is my life! God has something very special for my future, so I must remain close to him so I will not miss it. I learned that it takes mental discipline, not just emotions, to remain faithful to that walk. It takes time with God to be a Christian. These words, written by William Longstaff for a hymn which I keep in my Bible, describe it best:

Take time to be holy, the world rushes on;
Spend much time in secret with Jesus alone;

By looking to Jesus, like Him thou shalt be;
Thy friends in thy conduct His likeness shall see.

I learned in high school that the Christian life is a daily walk. As I have now begun my life as an adult, I plan to follow the "path of the righteous," which "is like the first gleam of dawn, shining ever brighter till the full light of day" (Proverbs 4:18). I will be a shining Christian until God brings his perfect will for my life into complete fullness.

Effective youth ministers follow in the footsteps of Jesus Christ, who had a clear sense of strategy, method and program in his ministry. The most important thing to note about Jesus' ministry is his care for and commitment to people: "When he saw the crowds, he had compassion on them, because they were harassed and helpless, like sheep without a shepherd" (Matthew 9:36). The Messiah also strategically spent time and energy discipling the twelve: "These twelve Jesus sent out with the following instructions ..." (Matthew 10:5). Last, the Master concentrated on training three individuals for future leadership: ". . . [Jesus] took Peter, John and James with him and went up onto a mountain to pray" (Luke 9:28).

The heart and genius of our Lord's ministry was the simple yet powerful way he gave himself in love to the crowds and to individuals: ". . . just as the Son of Man did not come to be served, but to serve, and to give his life as a ransom for many" (Matthew 20:28). This relational, incarnational, disciple-oriented approach to ministry moves across socio-economic classes, denominational preferences, group sizes, and programmatic styles to meet people where they are with the love of God.

Several years ago, while serving as Spiritual Life Director/Chaplain at Tyler Street Christian Academy in inner-city Dallas, I longed to reach the street-wise youth in our school. These young people were not about to attend any of our school or church programs voluntarily. Gradually, however, by showing these young men attention, taking them hunting and fishing, and making small talk in the hall and cafeteria, I forged some of the most fascinating relationships of my life.

Eventually, we began eating lunch together every Tuesday. We called this group the "Outlaws." My definition for this term was "*out* from [under] the *law* of sin and death" (Romans 8:2). I think the boys had other definitions for our group's name.

My love for these guys and my passion for them to know Christ as their Savior deepened with every encounter. Our conversations ranged from basics of the Christian faith to God's views on fighting, sex and drugs. I remember vividly the first time Sam Johnson (not his real name) understood the gospel. He exclaimed, "Oh! I know what you're saying: God knocked the hell out of Jesus so we could be saved." Though I wouldn't have chosen his words, I was thrilled that God's truth was becoming clear and exciting to this young man.

I don't know where the Outlaws are today spiritually. But I am convinced that two years of relational ministry will never completely lose its effects on those lovable rascals. I know I am richer for the experience.

This relational approach to ministry certainly cannot guarantee total success in reaching every youth. Nor does it assure you that every youth in your group will become a spiritual giant. Nevertheless, relational ministry is a biblical approach that, when coupled with solid, discipleship-oriented programming, is consistently effective. Countless youth and youth workers testify to the practicality and durability of this style of youth ministry. Here is what a few of them have to say:

> Relationally getting in contact with youth, getting to know their needs and their culture and thereby maximizing ministry to them is indeed the heart of youth ministry.
>
> *Duffy Robbins, Chair of Youth Ministry Dept.,
> Eastern College, St. Davids, PA.*

> Everything is being targeted to younger and younger audiences—education, drugs, career decisions, sex, movies and advertising.
>
> The Church has no choice but to deal with the faith of teenagers and even younger children.

To overlook or only give token support of discipleship-oriented, incarnational ministries to these
young people, is to ignore the great commission.

James Loftin, Minister of Youth
Christ UMC, Memphis, TN.

Impressing people is usually done at a distance. Im-
pacting people is usually done close up. To get close
to someone demands a relationship. The question we
face in the church today is, do we want to impress or
impact? I believe Christ would have us do the latter.
My most meaningful times of ministry have been when
I chose to get close to a group, revealing my true self—
joys, anxieties, frustrations, laughter, temper, as well
as my faith in Christ. In revealing myself, I have always found that others in turn reveal themselves.
When Christ is in the middle of all that revelation, lives
can be changed. I have never found the change to be
simply one way. It is always reciprocal. Their lives
change, and without a doubt, my life is changed too.
But that change always begins with a relationship.
In a world of microwave instant food and designer
lookalikes, people are crying out for something real
and lasting. We as the church need to commit to giving
a hungry world that "lasting stuff." However, in order
for that to come about, we have to be willing to take
the risk of building relationships with one another.

Joe Carmichael, Associate Pastor,
Tyler Street United Methodist Church, Dallas, TX.

As there is no substitute for a balanced family con-
sisting of a mother and father who love each other and
give structure to their children, there is no substitute
for an incarnational style of ministry in which the
youth pastor lives out his or her life in front of, and
over an extended period of time with, the young people
in the ministering group. There are crisis books and
films that you can read and see that give insight into
how to live the Christian life, but there is no substitute
for fleshing it out on a daily basis.
The most articulate, insightful and rewarding letter

THE HEART OF YOUTH MINISTRY

I have ever received was sent to me by a kid who grew up in our inner-city community, two blocks from the church, who overcame seemingly insurmountable odds in his own personal life. He is now married and will be graduating this spring with a Ph.D. in counseling, equipped to go into ministry and to be a positive force for the kingdom of God. His life is proof that relational ministry works.

Art Erickson, Associate Pastor,
Park Avenue United Methodist Church, Minneapolis, MN.

Relational, discipleship-oriented ministry was clearly Jesus' and the apostle Paul's approach for reaching and discipling people. However, when we attempt to apply these principles in the local church, a myriad of difficulties and obstacles arise: relationships are too time- and energy-consuming; youth groups often seem too large or too small; money and personnel are always in short supply; personalities and gifts don't seem to lend themselves to relational ministry; the church offers either no programming or too much programming; the youth culture is alien and even hostile; and some argue, "We've never done it that way." The list could go on and on.

This book addresses these difficulties with practical and proven solutions and suggestions. The book also provides you with:

■ A sound, experience-proven theological and philosophical framework for youth ministry;
■ Clear, workable insights;
■ Ideas and guidelines for successful relational ministry; and
■ Step-by-step instructions for building a youth program from the ground up that will meet youth where they are and move them toward Christian discipleship.

First, we'll look at some reasons why you as a pastor, youth professional, lay volunteer and/or parent should involve yourself in youth ministry.

CHAPTER

2

Youth Ministry No Luxury

Why Youth Ministry and Why Now?

By Jorge Acevedo

Budgets are tight. Personnel is scarce. Kids can be un-cooperative. Given these obstacles, why is youth ministry a necessity in the local church? This question must be asked—and answered.

Youth ministry is not an extravagant luxury that only "big" churches can do. Wherever youth exist, the church must seek to win them to Christ and disciple them. To fail to minister to youth is to ignore our scriptural mandate to close our eyes to the problems of today's young people.

The Biblical Picture

At the heart of the Bible, we find a loving God who seeks to be personally related to his creation. Sin alienated humanity from God, and so he devised a beautiful plan of redemption. This plan unfolded throughout the history of Israel. The Bible is the story of how God seeks to be related to his people. God personally called Abraham in Genesis 12. He commissioned Moses at the burning bush in Exodus 3. He called the boy Samuel by name in the middle of the night in 1 Samuel 3. These are only a few examples of how God seeks a personal relationship with his people.

try of Jesus, whom God in love and grace sent to live, die and rise again for individual sinners. Likewise, God wants us to be personally related to people. And although this relationship is not limited by age, sex or race, the Bible is clear that especially young people are to be taught about God. Moses reminds Israel to keep the commandments "so that you, your children and their children after them may fear the Lord your God . . ." (Deuteronomy 6:2). The "preacher" of Ecclesiastes, after declaring much of life "vanity," says at the end of the book, "Remember your Creator in the days of your youth . . ." (12:1a). Something about being young often makes people more receptive to God's message.

God has always used young people to fulfill his purposes. He called the young shepherd boy David to lead Israel to her glory days. Young Timothy was trained by Paul and used by God to pastor the church at Ephesus. God has used children and youth to lead nations, speak prophetic words, pastor churches and perform miracles. And God still wants to use young people in his Church today.

One of the most beautiful biblical examples of God's call on the life of a young person is the story of Jesus at the temple in Jerusalem recorded in Luke 2:41-52. Joseph and Mary were returning home from the Passover Feast in Jerusalem with twelve-year old Jesus (the age of a seventh grader) when the pre-teen became separated from his family. When his parents realized that Jesus was not with any of their friends or kinfolk, they frantically returned to Jerusalem to comb the streets looking for their son. After three prayer-filled, hectic days, they found the boy sitting in the temple talking to some teachers. His mother said to him, "Son, why have you treated us like this? Your father and I have been anxiously searching for you."

Jesus replied, "Why were you searching for me? Didn't you know I had to be in my Father's house?" Jesus' response reflects God's desire for all people, including teenagers. God wants a personal relationship with young people who are willing to say, in the midst of tremendous peer pressure, "I'm about my Father's affairs." He wants youth who won't bow down to the idols of their culture— who do not need to "sow their wild oats."

We, whom God has called to work with this precious commodity called youth, need to remember the biblical perspective—that God calls young people to a personal friendship with him to serve him in whatever environment he places them.

The Openness of Youth

Nine months after I became minister of youth at Trinity Hill United Methodist Church, Scott, a seventh grader, approached me after a Saturday night youth event. Almost reluctantly he asked me, "Jorge, what is all this stuff about a relationship with God?" We went into my office, and I told him how God wanted to have an intimate friendship with him. Scott told me that he did not have that kind of relationship with God but that he wanted one. We bowed our heads, and Scott asked God to be his Lord and Savior.

When I was a youth counselor at Pine Castle United Methodist Church in Orlando, Florida, I developed a relationship with a high school student named Stewart. He was a quiet, polite young man who was dissatisfied with his life. He attended Sunday night youth meetings consistently, and our friendship developed. For months Stewart said, "I want a relationship with Jesus, but I want it to really change my life and the way I live it." One Sunday night a missionary from Korea, Keith Brown, was speaking. God was moving in my heart, and I went to the altar to pray. I had just knelt down when Stewart tapped me on the shoulder and with tears running down his cheeks said, "Jorge, it's time. I want to be a Christian."

Scott and Stewart are only two examples of young people's openness to spiritual things.

Teenagers live in a highly complex, changing world. From ages twelve to eighteen they undergo a tremendous transformation. The physical changes that accompany puberty's onset alter the way young people perceive life. Their entry onto the junior or senior high campus creates a social change as they face dating, driving and jobs. Often teenagers act tough, yet harbor complex internal feelings and thoughts.

During this time of tremendous upheaval, youth are spiritually hungry and open to the gospel. Eighty-five percent of all people who receive Christ do so before the age of nineteen.[1] This is a phenomenal statistic. Yet almost all of our time, effort and money is used to reach adults. Youth are open to the gospel, but are we taking advantage of their openness?

In the March 1984 *Religion in America* Gallup report, the Princeton Religion Research Center, Inc., reported some amazing facts about the American teenager. For example, nineteen percent of teenagers surveyed said they were "evangelical," meaning they had had a born-again experience, they encouraged others to accept Christ, or they believed that the Bible is not mistaken in its teaching.[2] This means that nearly one-fifth of junior and senior high students consider themselves evangelicals. These students could have an astronomical impact on their campuses and churches. Also, the same poll found that forty percent of American teenagers said that religious beliefs are very important; twenty-two percent said these beliefs are most important in their lives.

Wes was a starter on Lexington's Tates Creek High School football team. He asked his coach if he could pray with the team before the games. The coach agreed. At the last home game, when seniors are honored, Wes' teammates asked him to pray the opening prayer before the crowds. What a thrill to hear a young disciple of Jesus Christ pray before hundreds! Wes is only one member of God's team of young men and women who are committed to living for him on their high school campuses.

The Gallup report also found that eighty-seven percent of teenagers polled said they pray, and thirty-nine percent said they pray frequently.[3] This means that even in their high-pressure world the American teenager is discovering that turning one's eyes and voice toward heaven brings peace. The fact that most kids pray also means something within them yearns to reach out and commune with God.

I've found this to be true in our Sunday evening youth meetings, which close with a time of worship. We turn out the lights in the basement and light a large white candle, called our "sharing candle." The youth know that this is a time for them to share anything, including prayer requests. I'm always amazed when sixty junior and senior high school students share their joys and heartaches. Both tears and laughter are a part of this special time. As we move to prayer, the youth pray for their friends' needs and thank God for blessings. Contrary to what some adults believe, youth like to pray. We cannot use the excuse that youth "aren't interested" to avoid ministering to them. Behind the anger and rebellion many youth display lies a dormant seed of spiritual life waiting to be watered by the living water that Jesus offers. If the church will invest in youth ministry that is intentional, relational and discipleship-oriented, multitudes of teenagers will be won to Christ and nurtured into disciples. Today's youth are open to the gospel of Jesus Christ. Are our local churches open to them?

The Troubled World of Youth

All one needs to do is quickly browse through the newspaper, walk through the mall, or talk to a parent of a teenager to realize that youth are in trouble. The statistics are horrifying, but observing the lives of real teenagers is heart breaking. Talking to youth who abuse drugs, alcohol and sex can leave you with a feeling of hopelessness. We, who are the church, have the answer in Jesus.

I believe the biggest problem facing teenagers is the breakdown of the home. With the divorce rate at nearly fifty percent, the family structure and support system that youth need is quickly fading away. Consider the following statistics from *Youth Worker Update*[4]:

■ One out of two marriages in the United States ends in divorce—the highest rate in the world, nearly double that of Sweden, the runner up.

■ Twenty-six percent of children now live in a single-parent household.

■ Thirty-five percent of American children live in step-relationships (i.e. child and parent with a partner who is not the child's biological parent. Many children live in double step-relationships—Mom has a new man, Dad has a new lady).

■ It is predicted that sixty percent of children born today will spend part of their lives in a single-parent household and in one or more step-relationships.

■ More than seventy million Americans are currently living in step-relationships, whether the couples are married, dating or living with a partner.

■ Sixty percent of second marriages fail.

■ It has been predicted that seventy-five percent of all step-relationships will break up. The major causes of these breakups are child and step-relationship issues.

■ By 1990 more people will be in a second marriage than a first.

The church must address these problems. No youth group can avoid the fact that many of its kids come from broken homes. And many of the families that are still together could be classified as broken because they spend little time communicating or being together as a family, have workaholic parents or lack any reasonable and consistent discipline.

With the family in such disarray, it is easy to understand why teen suicide, drug and alcohol abuse, stress, depression and sexual promiscuity are rampant. However, amid the chaos of modern life, the church can offer a stable and ethical setting for youth. Although the church can never entirely replace the family, it must often act as a surrogate home for troubled teens. Youth workers can be temporary substitute parents who give love and consistency.

Planned Parenthood released a Harris Poll which found that fifty-seven percent of seventeen-year-olds have had sexual intercourse; seventy-three percent of girls and fifty percent of boys said peer pressure is the chief reason for sexual activity.[5] It is obvious that the sexual activity of our youth is out of control. The church is needed more than ever to provide an environment where the biblical perspective on sexual behavior is taught and modeled.

Teenagers often drop by my office "just to talk." After some light conversation, the visit's real agenda inevitably emerges. A date with a friend got too "hot and heavy," and they had intercourse. Every youth worker who has heard this sad story knows that statistics have faces. They are no longer cold facts. They are some of "my kids." As a friend and minister, you can help them find God's healing and forgiveness; you have the privilege of teaching them about God's standards for sexuality.

Drug abuse is another all-too-real problem. Susan (not her real name) stopped by the youth office during the summer I was an intern at Pine Castle. She said she wanted to become a Christian. We talked to her about giving up drugs and alcohol to follow God, and she agreed. With a thud she plunked a bag of pills and two packs of cigarettes on the desk. We flushed the pills down the toilet and threw her cigarettes in the trash can.

Unfortunately, after we prayed Susan left the office and, despite her good intentions, bought a new pack of cigarettes and more drugs later that same day. Susan is only one of the thousands of teenagers who turns to drugs and alcohol to ease the pain or to fit into the crowd.

Whether a teenager is burdened by a family breakdown, sexual promiscuity or drug and alcohol abuse, the Church of Jesus Christ has the opportunity and responsibility to offer that youth a sound biblical perspective. As Christians, we can help youth avoid these pitfalls and find healing and forgiveness after tragedies occur.

Hope for the Church

We often hear the cliché that the youth of today are the church of tomorrow. I believe that the youth of today are the church of tomorrow *and* today. The church needs to raise up a generation of young people who are grounded in God's Word, committed to his church and willing to serve a broken and lost world. The church's new frontier is the junior and senior high campuses of this world.

Of my denomination's 9.1 million members, 589,687 youth attended Sunday school in 1986. It's exciting to consider that in my denomination alone we have more than half a million youth with whom to work. The impact this army could have for Jesus Christ is mind-boggling.

But as encouraging as this thought is, we must also note that 3.5 percent of my denomination's young people, or more than twenty thousand youth, quit coming to Sunday school in 1986. Why? Was it because of poor curriculum or political struggles in the church? I don't think so. I believe it is more likely that twenty thousand youth quit coming because of inadequately trained youth workers, both lay and clergy. The exodus of youth from Sunday school might be blamed on our inability to teach them that the gospel of Jesus Christ can have meaning, even in their world of peer pressure, abortions, R-rated movies and MTV.

In their prophetic book, *Rekindling the Flame*, William Willimon and Robert Wilson tell how the United Methodist Church, like many denominations, has fallen prey to the sin of accommodation. They write:

> *One of our current sources of membership loss is our inability to retain our young people, after their maturity, in our church. When they become adults, too many of our children leave the United Methodist Church for other denominations, while others drop out of the church altogether. Decades of haphazard Christian education, the ethics of cultural accommodation, non-biblical preaching, and neglect of the task of formation have left us with a bitter harvest.*[6]

The church's hope rests squarely in the laps of our teenagers. The future of the church depends on our transferring the faith to our young people. The success of a youth ministry depends upon how willing the youth minister is to actively participate in teen's lives and help them become disciples of Jesus Christ, applying Scripture to their lives. In the following chapters we will tell you how young people can become world-changers through a relational and discipleship-oriented youth ministry style.

Getting the Big Picture

The Theory Behind Relational, Discipleship-Oriented Youth Ministry

By Hule Goddard

I'll never forget the first time I went deer hunting with my uncle. I'd spent time in the forest all of my life, but I had never been able to see a deer in the forest. That morning I heard an animal scurrying through the forest. I looked wildly into the twilight, wanting to shoot at something, but I had no idea what my target was.

Not many years after that, I had my first opportunity to shoot at a buck. It ran out into the field and turned broadside. I can still remember watching the steam rise from the animal's fur on that cold December morning. Caught up in "buck fever," I saw the deer with my eyes but kept my gun pointed at the ground. I fired the gun and tore up the ground in front of me! I missed because I failed to aim the barrel of my rifle toward the deer.

Often our approaches to ministry are like these hunting experiences. We feel called into the ministry. We are anxious. We have a vital relationship with God and long to help other people, but we don't know what a "deer in the woods" looks like. We've never done ministry and don't know exactly what it should look like—much less how to do it! Even those of us who have a clear picture of what we ought to do often begin without a sense of direction. We shoot wildly, hoping that we'll hit something. The old adage describes this situation: "To fail to plan is to plan to fail."

I remember the first deer I killed. Somebody must have tied the animal down because it stood still for so long. I had time to calm myself and review the techniques needed to make a clean shot—to inhale about a half breath and hold it, to hold the gun steady, to squeeze the trigger gently instead of pulling it. The deer was squarely in my scope, and it was an easy target. I felt joy because it took only one shot; I had done what I set out to accomplish and had done it well. And I think that God calls us to aim for specific goals and reach them.

The old adage, "Aim at nothing and you'll surely hit it," rings true for youth ministry. In this chapter, we'll explore ways to take aim as we develop relationships with young people and give them direction in their Christian lives.

The Context of Youth Ministry

God's Call to Evangelize (Come Level)

Throughout the Scriptures we read how God has been reaching out to men and women. Since man's initial sin in the garden, God's call has been, "Come to me. Seek my face. Turn to me and be related to me." From the days of Israel until today, God has drawn and called sinful people to himself. The most dramatic example of this is God's coming to earth as Jesus Christ and living among us as a man. It's amazing how far God will go to reach us. The all-powerful creator came, washed men's feet and died on a criminal's cross. This should convince us that one of our major concerns should be evangelism. If the cross says anything to us, it says that God was willing to go to whatever extent necessary to save humankind.

One of God's passions is to reach persons where they are—in their pain and sin, in their brokenness and hunger. In the Great Commission, Jesus says, "go and make disciples of all nations, baptizing them in the name of the Father and of the Son and of the Holy Spirit, and teaching them to obey everything I have commanded you. And surely I will be with you always, to the very end of the age" (Matthew 28:19-20). We, then, must reach out to teenagers where they are.

God's Call to Teach His Ways (Grow Level)

How are we to relate to God and to each other? How should we deal with our sexuality? Our identity? Our role in the world? Our economics? God wants to teach us his ways so our lives will have a sense of meaning and justice.

In the Torah we learn about God through Moses and Joshua. Deuteronomy 4 clearly explains that we ought to learn from God's commands and teach them to our children.

Our Lord's earthly ministry also centered around teaching. In the Sermon on the Mount, the parables and throughout the Gospels we find that God is teaching us. Acts 6 tells how the apostles ordained deacons to distribute food and care for widows, thus freeing the apostles for proclaiming the word and teaching. Teaching was a priority of Jesus and the early church, and it should be a priority in youth ministry.

God's Call to Raise Up Disciples (Disciple Level)

God is never satisfied with mere talk or glib confession. One of Jesus' most stinging rebukes appears in Matthew 15:8. He told the Pharisees they fit the description in Isaiah 29:13: "These people . . . honor me with their lips, but their hearts are far from me." So often this describes the church and individual Christians. We know what to do but have difficulty using our knowledge of God in our lifestyles.

Yet, as we study the Bible, we find a major concern of God's is that we help disciple others. (A classic example is young Elisha spending time with Elijah.) The older prophet did not just talk about God's ways but lived in them. Elisha learned to follow God by patterning himself after his mentor. Similarly, young Joshua spent time with Moses, not only to see God's glory and to hear about God's great principles, but also to learn to walk with God and to know God as Moses did. This prepared Joshua to effectively lead the people. Another biblical example of this kind of hands-on teaching is Jesus' discipling of the twelve. Jesus taught the twelve disciples God's ways by demonstration, involving them in ministry and holding them accountable. We must demonstrate ministry to our young pepole, actively involve them in ministry and hold them accountable for their Christian youth.

God's Call for Leaders (Leadership Training)

Jesus also spent special time with the three, Peter, James and John, to prepare them for leadership. God has always raised up men and women who have a unique purpose, who aren't satisfied to merely know God themselves but who are called to make a difference in their world. They are disciples who take the Great Commission seriously. They want to make God's kingdom, with its peace, order, equity, salvation and perfect communion with God, a living reality in their own lives, their families, churches, work places, political systems and the world.

The Scriptures record a "hall of fame" (Hebrews 11) of men and women whom God developed into leaders. For example, we can read about Abraham's ups and downs as God went to great lengths to prepare him to be the father of the nation of Israel. In the New Testament, we learn how Jesus nurtured Peter and taught him how to reach and disciple people. After Peter was restored and filled with the Holy Spirit, he boldly carried out that ministry. We must teach young people to be disciplers of others.

Goals for Ministry

As we've seen, God has a desire for evangelization, Christian growth, discipleship and leadership development. These form the general context within which we minister to people. Our goal should be God's goal, that is, to produce mature men and women who love God and love other people. After all, Christians are not called to live a narcissistic, self-satisfying existence while waiting to go to heaven. Rather, we are called to be in touch with God and with other people.

Our approach to youth ministry begins with Jesus' response to the Pharisees who asked him, "Teacher, which is the greatest commandment in the Law?" Jesus replied, "'Love the Lord your God with all you heart and with all your soul and with all your mind.' This is the first and greatest commandment. And the second is like it: 'Love your neighbor as yourself'" (Matthew 22:36-39). This theme echoes throughout the Scriptures—from the Torah to the Prophets to the Gospels, in the book of Acts and throughout the Epistles. We find it in the writings of the early church fathers, in the reformation, in the Wesleyan revivals and in the early camp meetings in America. Today we still hear it from our pulpits time and time again. This theme sums up our faith: we are called to love God and to love humankind.

The Role of the Family and the Church

In addition to God's call on our lives, other elements help form the context of youth ministry. One of these is the family. God says that we are to care for our families and to nurture our children in ways that will bring health and abundant life. In 1 Timothy 3:4-5, the apostle Paul gives us a clear picture of desirable family life as he describes requirements for those who want to serve in the church. Paul indicates that the primary institution for evangelism, teaching, discipleship and leadership training is the family. In effect, he is telling those of us who aspire to be church leaders, elders and pastors: "Get your own household in order. If you cannot nurture your own family in Christ, you have no business trying to do so in the house of God." And to re-emphasize this point, in 1 Timothy 5:8 Paul says, "If anyone does not provide for his relatives, and especially for his immediate family, he has denied the faith and is worse than an unbeliever." Paul says that for us to neglect our own family is a blatant denial of our faith. It's a denial of God's unconditional love and commitment.

Jesus' earthly life gives us another beautiful example of God's commitment to the family. Jesus apparently spent thirty years providing for his family. Surely he could have begun his ministry at a younger age, but perhaps because of his culture Jesus needed to stay home those years. He could have accomplished much in his twenties, but God the Son chose to stay home, working with his family, being faithful to his commitment, possibly because his father had passed away and he was the oldest son. Thus Jesus demonstrated for us the incredible importance of our family and of nurturing in the home.

The context of our youth ministry also contains God's great commitment to his people. In the Old Testament, "his people" was the nation of Israel. In the New Testament, "his people" was the fledgling church.

In John 17 Christ prays for the church and for our unity, that we would become one so that the world might know that he is the Messiah. In John 13:35, Jesus told the disciples that "All men will know that you are my disciples if you love one another." Ephesians 4 tells how believers are joined in one body in Christ, with each part of the body (each person) using his or her individual gifts. This is the dynamic by which spiritual growth takes place.

God brings people to himself primarily through the human family and through the spiritual family, the church. These help form the context in which we are called to do our youth ministry.

The Spiritual Womb

I'll never forget when our first child was in Loretta's womb. This child was eight days late, and we were *so* ready for her to come forth! We had so many dreams, goals and plans for this little one. When the day came for Sarah Jo to be born, our excitement and trepidation quickly gave way to old-fashioned hard work. As Loretta endured those tedious and very intense hours of labor, each minute seemed like centuries to her. At times everything else in the world lost its significance. The labor of bringing forth that little one was the only reality. Our daughter's first cries brought an end to our anxiety and a flood of joy and excitement. Little did we know that our real labor was just beginning.

I think that's where we find ourselves as youth ministers. We are called to help in the delivery, just as the obstetrician helped bring our daughter into the world.

In fact, labor and childbirth illustrate the big picture we are studying in this chapter as we explore how God, families and the church work together to bring wholeness and and maturity in the lives of people.

How the Holy Spirit and the Family Aid Christian Maturation

The chart on page 41 shows a "spiritual womb," which

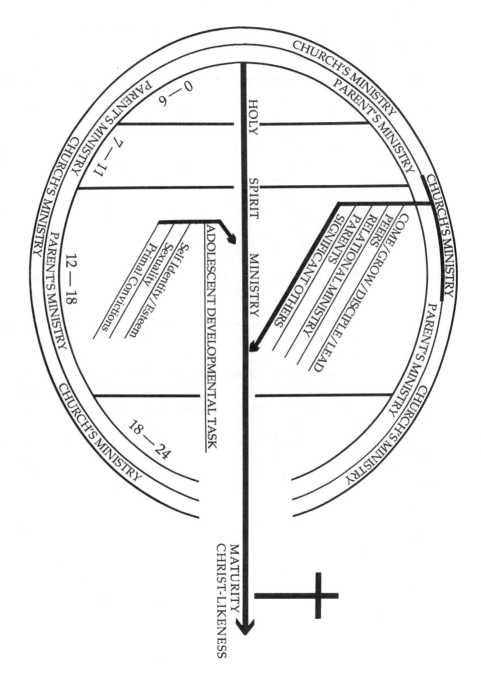

can help us understand the Christian's developmental stages. The thin line in the middle of the chart is our lifeline, if you will, representing the time from when we are born until the day we die. Throughout this time, the Holy Spirit works to call us to God, to help us grow in our understanding of God and our Christian faith and to give us insight and perspective. The Holy Spirit strives to bring us into an incarnational experience of the Word of God, a lifestyle of Christian living. The Holy Spirit also wants to give us a servant's heart so that we realize we are saved to serve. We are called to incarnate the phrase from the Lord's Prayer that the kingdom of God would come to our world, wherever we find ourselves.

The outside of the spiritual womb is covered by the body of Christ, the ministry of the church. (We youth workers are a vital part of the church's ministry.) Why is the church outside the womb? Because God's first line of ministry is the Holy Spirit, then the family. Therefore, inside the womb, around the lifeline but just outside the Holy Spirit's ministry, is the family's ministry.

Any family that cares at all for its young person will tend to have the same sort of developmental goals as the Holy Spirit. Christian parents work, from the time a child is born, to bring that child into a living, active relationship with the Lord Jesus. Parents help young people grow, not only spiritually, but also emotionally, academically, socially and in every way possible.

Christian parents are actively involved in helping their young person develop a Christian lifestyle—a lifestyle that reflects one's love for God and a desire to be disciplined by his laws and his *agape* love. The family also labors to help a young person develop the ability to share, to be a servant and to use his or her gifts and talents in a meaningful life and vocation. The Christian parents we youth ministers work with have the goal of seeing young persons become mature, Christlike, world-changing Christians—the same goal the Holy Spirit has for youth.

How the Church Aids Christian Growth

So what role does the church play in youth ministry? As we've seen, the outer line that surrounds the womb in our

42

illustration represents the ministry of the church. The church, therefore, should work in harmony with the goals of the Holy Spirit and the family.

When young children are born to moms and dads in the church, the church focuses on helping the parents come to God and commit themselves to him. The church can provide practical ministry to harried new moms and dads (who may have been up all night caring for little children) by giving them moms' days out and nurseries during the services. Such programs allow the church to minister to both children and adults in early years.

As children reach ages seven to eleven and begin to develop greater comprehension skills, the church must design ministries to introduce them to God and call them to an initial commitment. Children can learn to adopt God's perspectives and be disciplined in the ways of God. Jesus said, "Forbid them not, for of such is the kingdom of God" (Mark 10:14-16). Thus we plant the seeds of Christian leadership.

Next comes the stage of development known as the adolescent period. In our illustration we will divide it into two areas. Many psychologists divide it into three periods—early adolescence (usually considered between eleven and fourteen), middle adolescence (fifteen through sixteen or seventeen) and late adolescence (generally eighteen through twenty-four). But for our purposes, we will just divide this stage into what we will call early adolescence and late adolescence.

Adolescents' Three Developmental Tasks

During early adolescence, a young person undergoes the second most dramatic change of his or her entire life (the first being the time between zero and two.) They change physically, emotionally, spiritually and socially.

Keith Olson, in his book *Counseling Teenagers*, defines three primary developmental tasks that young people perform during early adolescence. The first is to build self-identity and a healthy sense of self-esteem. The second is to build a healthy sense of sexuality. The third developmental task essential for healthy adulthood is to build a set of primal convictions or basic beliefs.

Olson identified these tasks from studies that have been done by Piaget, Sullivan, Jung, Kolberg and other psychologists who gave us a wealth of knowledge about adolescent development. So let us take a moment to examine these tasks.

Developing Self-Identity. As sure as geese fly south in the winter, a young person who reaches the age of puberty will begin to develop a sense of independence and self-identity. Younger children gain self-esteem from parents, teachers and coaches who tell them when they perform well that they are good and important and have this or that gift and ability. But as adolescents journey into adulthood they begin to build an intrinsic sense of self-esteem, a self-identity that they choose, not one that is assigned to them.

Young people use several mirrors during this era of life to judge how they look and feel about themselves. One important mirror young people bring with them from childhood is Mom and Dad. Now this mirror is not as key as it was in childhood, when it was the most significant mirror, but it is still vitally important. Parents cannot afford to withdraw their unconditional love, positive affirmation and honest evaluation during an adolescent's years.

Another mirror that young people look into, and the most-used mirror during this stage, is peer influence. They look to each other to help them discover who they are and what values they will have. It ought to scare us to death that most of our adolescents are establishing their self-esteem based on what other young people think about them.

A third mirror that young people use to build their self-esteem and to gain a sense of their own value is the opinion of significant others—adults such as coaches, pastors, teachers, trusted relatives and even rock musicians and movie stars. Young people look into this mirror to see what those adults reflect as valuable and worthy. Adolescents are sensitive to these adults' attitudes and reactions toward them as they develop their identities.

Developing a Healthy Sexuality. Another developmental task Olson identifies is to build a healthy sense of sexuality. During early adolescence children's bodies begin to bloom into adulthood. As they mature in every dimension, development of secondary sex characteristics is especially strong. As the mysterious and wonderful gift of sexuality explodes within young people, they must somehow figure out how to handle it.

Again, young people look to the various mirrors to understand their own sexuality and to decide what are healthy and unhealthy ways to express it. It is vitally important that young people have Mom and Dad, off of whom they may bounce different ideas. Parents should be healthy mirrors at this point in young people's lives.

Of course, another mirror youth look into to develop their sense of sexuality is their peers, and that is terrifying! Young people are forming their sexual identities in a culture laden with hedonistic, self-centered, narcissistic sex. They look to the movies, television, advertising and what other young people are saying about sex. Youth also look to significant other adults for signals about what is healthy and what is not.

Developing Primal Convictions. The third developmental task that Olson defines is that young people must formulate their primal convictions. Throughout their childhood, youth have been taught their parents' beliefs, church's beliefs, relatives' beliefs and school's beliefs. Generally, childhood is not a time of questioning such values. However, as they enter early adulthood, young people must decide for themselves what they believe and why they believe it.

Again, young people look into the mirror of what Mom and Dad believe (both verbally and with their lifestyles). They also use peers as a primary mirror, asking: "What do my peers believe about God? What are their reactions toward faith in God, or do they even have faith in God?" Youth look to the culture and the significant others in the culture, such as politicians or stars or television preachers. Pastors are also significant others that youth watch as they formulate their primal convictions.

For many youth, this working out of basic beliefs continues well into late adolescence or early adulthood. During the process, they sometimes step away from the faith. They may stop attending church. They may start asking extremely difficult and challenging questions.

Practical Ministry to Adolescents

So how can we as a church, in harmony with the Holy Spirit and the family, minister to young people as they take these important developmental steps that set the course of their adult lives? After all, it is much easier to set one's compass in God's direction at the dawn of adulthood than to change direction years later.

Effective Youth Programming (Come, Grow, Disciple Leadership Training)

I propose that we involve ourselves in the same sort of ministry in which parents are involved. First, we must offer our young people come level ministry (see chapter four)—programs and relational ministry that call youth to genuine commitment to Jesus Christ as Lord. We must interpret and give reasons for our faith in God and suggest reasons why youth should believe in Christianity for themselves.

I believe we also ought to provide our young people with an effective grow level ministry (see chapter five), including Bible studies and retreats. This helps them understand the relevance of God's Word and his message to their self-identity, their sexuality and their basic beliefs. Youth need to hear our reasons for our belief in God, Jesus as the Son of God and the Scriptures as the inspired Word of God.

I also feel it is imperative for us as a church to offer young people genuine discipleship opportunities (see chapter six), so they can build relationships with God that become a fourth, most important, mirror. They can use this mirror of their relationship with God and his Word to determine how to think about themselves, how their sexuality should develop and what their primal beliefs ought to be.

We also need to allow young people to learn what it means to be a Christian leader. At this very early stage of adulthood, we must guide their hearts toward sharing themselves for the glory of God and for the good of the world.

Ministry to Parents, Peers and Significant Others

Parental/Family Ministry. We need to perform a ministry to parents as part of our overall ministry to adolescents. We need to help moms and dads interpret the struggles and processes of adolescence and form support groups to help each other. Much agony and conflict occurs at home as young people decide that many of the things that were so precious to them in childhood are signs of immaturity. Adolescents tend to clam up and not talk to their parents or to be argumentative. So it is important that we have an effective ministry to parents to help them be useful mirrors for young people.

Creating a Christian Peer Mirror. Also, one of the best ministries we can offer young people is to create for them a group of Christian peers. A Christian peer group is a mirror that reflects back to our young people: "You are worth much—you are valuable to us." This group can generate the unconditional love that is essential for healthy development of one's personality and self-esteem. It can say, "It is okay to be a Christian; it is a good thing to do God's will." This peer group can also provide a healthy attitude toward sexuality, or at least a healthier one than what they will get at school, asserting the belief that sex is something worth waiting for.

The Role of Godly Significant Others. Finally, we can provide our young people with another valuable mirror— Christian significant others. These can be laypeople, people on our ministry team, our own youth ministry, our pastor or adults who are successful in their fields who have given their lives to God. Such adults provide living examples so our young people can say, "This is the result of following Jesus." As youth ministers and pastors we can affirm young people, affirm their faith, affirm a Christian view of sexuality and affirm God's call in their lives.

One Bottom Line: To Produce World Changers

Through the labor of the Holy Spirit, parents and the body of Christ, we want to see our young people walk out of our youth groups as mature as they can be at age eighteen. We want them to be world-changing disciples, to see their vocation as a ministry, to become effectors rather than just conductors of what is going on, to see their lives as a mission, to be self-starters in their relationships with

God and to have a sense of God's perspective. The apostle Paul described this goal in Ephesians 4:12-13,

". . . that the body of Christ may be built up until we all reach unity in the faith and in the knowledge of the Son of God and become mature, attaining to the whole measure of the fullness of Christ."

To this end we all labor and strive, but to be successful, we must see the big picture of what we are doing in youth ministry.

Relational Ministry

One of our most important ministries to young people is relational ministry. This gives us an opportunity to spend time with youth, building bridges of friendship, so that during the stormy days and nights of adolescence they will have a safe adult with whom to talk. Youth need someone with whom to discuss ideas, to cry and to hold. They need someone to help them understand themselves, God, the body of Christ and parents.

Funnel Ministry

Relational, discipleship-oriented youth ministry centers on God's families' basic desire for youth and the developmental and cultural needs of teens. We use a funnel graph (see page 49) to illustrate this type of ministry.

You will note that the illustration includes each of the goals of ministry. By using this funnel illustration as a guide, we can give focus and definition to our activities, programs and relational ministry. Thus, our ministry is less likely to be just shooting blindly in the woods or with unfocused rapid-fire. The system the funnel represents can help us realize our goal of ministering to youth where they are and moving them toward discipleship.

As we guide young people through the funnel's developmental process, we find that each year we cannot graduate hundreds or even tens, but only a few. In our local program at Wilmore UMC, our goal is to graduate six youth who have completed all the funnel's levels. But we know this handful of individuals are well on their way to being the world-changing, mature, young adults that God desires. He can

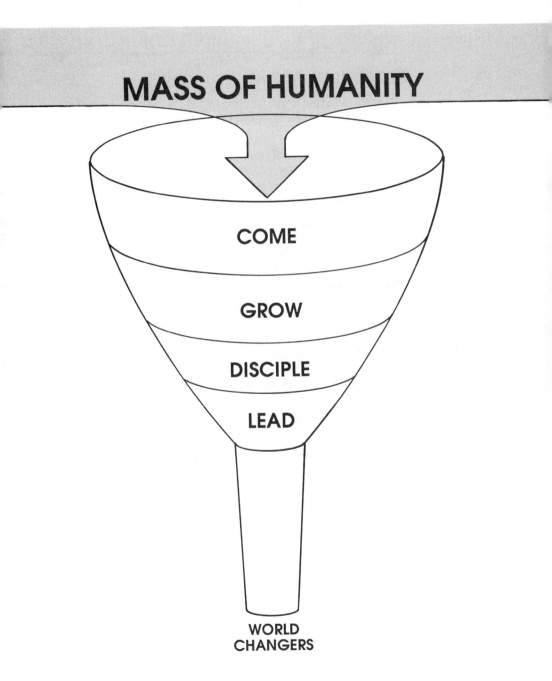

use these young Moseses, Joshuas and Peters to bring our world the revolutionary change for which the Lord Jesus died on the cross for everyone to have.

A Case Study: Brad and Annie Fairchild

The lives of Brad and Annie Fairchild, who were members of the youth group at Tyler Street United Methodist Church, illustrate how this "funnel ministry" works. Here are their personal testimonies:

Annie Fairchild

I've been a Christian all my life, or so it seems. I am fortunate to have grown up in a Christian home with two wonderful, loving parents.

But even though I was in a Christian home, I could feel my Christian life, at times, becoming stagnant. I needed some role models outside of the home whom I could look to for leadership and direction.

My church youth group filled this role for me when I was in high school. Under the leadership of Hule Goddard and senior pastor Paul Morell, I experienced a reawakening in my spiritual life. The three areas that had the greatest impact on me were (1) the leadership council, (2) the emphasis on praise and worship and (3) the small discipleship group.

The leadership council was a relatively small group of individuals who desired to be leaders. Here we were challenged to become more like Christ in different areas of our lives. One of these areas was our personal devotions with Christ. Because of my experience in the youth group, this has become very important to me. Each day I spend time with God, reading his Word and praying to him. I believe I can accept more of his strength and joy than I could if we did not have good communications. Another benefit of the leadership council was an assignment on one of our leadership retreats to prepare a lesson for the whole group. This not only made me research my topic but also made me appreciate others who give lessons because I know what time they spend preparing them.

Today I love to praise and worship, but I never really did this until I came to Tyler Street. Usually, each youth meeting would open with singing and worship. Even when I was having a bad day, I would make myself sing and things would turn around. I still enjoy singing those songs during my personal time with God. It is so refreshing.

The third factor that helped me grow in the Lord during high school was my discipleship group. Once a week about five girls would meet for fellowship and to learn how to be godly women. At the end of each evening we would think of something for which to hold each other accountable during the next week. This system kept us traveling on the right pathways.

The Holy Spirit became more and more real to me as my leaders focused my attention on him and what he could do in my life if he had complete control.

I graduated from Liberty University in May 1988. At LU, I also grew considerably, and I expect to continue growing as a Christian throughout the years. Today, the Holy Spirit does have control over my life.

Brad Fairchild

I was raised in a Christian home and became a Christian at a very early age. But when I was in the eighth grade I began to fall under peer pressure. I did not totally reject God, but I was living two lives. My parents and grandmother thought I was living a perfectly angelic life, while at school I was in with the wrong crowd.

Summer came and I was away from my school friends. Therefore I spent more time with church activities and Christian friends. That summer I recommitted my life to Christ and began to grow as a Christian.

My freshman year at high school began at a Christian academy. It was the start of a new life. Before school began I decided to strive to live a strong Christian life and find quality friends. The Lord fulfilled my *desire. Having good Christian friends was vital to my success in living a Christian life in high school.*

Quality fellowship through good youth activities was important in developing these relationships. For instance, we had a Bible study in a small group that was highly committed to attendance. I grew and learned many useful things in that Bible study. There was also leadership and youth council. Here we were given responsibility for youth events, meetings and Sunday school. We learned how to lead and plan these activities. Today, I still use those skills. We also took backpacking, skiing and camping trips, which enhanced our physical, spiritual and mental growth. My most memorable trip was going to Colorado for a ten day stress camp. It was very physical with plenty of backpacking, rock climbing and other outdoor activities. We carried all of our supplies for the ten days on our backs. Trips like these build character.

Many activities and teachings during those years helped me to grow. I learned how to make daily Bible study more exciting and fulfilling, and I am still learning. Having prayer with my girlfriend, who is my wife today, is another valuable practice I began in high school. My high school years were essential in bringing me close to the Lord. I thank God for these good younger years and am looking forward to many more years of growing closer to him.

We youth ministers are giving our lives for young men and women like Brad and Annie. To that end, we work with every young person we can reach.

Facing Some Limitations

We should mention at the outset that it's not our responsibility for every young person to come to Christ or grow or disciple or lead. Only God can bring that kind of growth. Our responsibility is to meet young people where they are, to love them and to offer them relational ministry. We are to guide them through our program (the funnel) as far as they will go in their journeys towards being the people God wants them to be.

Usually, we can't neatly classify any individual young person as a come level or disciple level youth. People are complex, beautiful and dynamic. One day a young person may be at the come level, another day be inching toward the grow level and then the next day be back to the come level. Some days our best young people will be miserable, self-centered piles of frustration and failure. Understanding this, we must use the information in the next few chapters as general guidelines, not as rigid formulas for relational ministry.

4 Come Level Ministry

Creating an Atmosphere to Lead Youth to Christ

By Hule Goddard

As we explained in the last chapter, the word "come" sig-nifies the entry-level ministry in our funnel. "Come" is a powerful verb. If we trace this little verb through the Gospels, we discover some interesting and powerful truths about God. The Gospels tell us that God comes to us in love. John 1:11 says, "He came to that which was his own, but his own did not receive him." In Mark 10:45, Jesus says of himself, "The Son of Man did not come to be served, but to serve, and to give his life as a ransom for many." God comes to us even in the pig pen of life, as we learn in the parable of the prodigal son in Luke 15. God comes to us where we are and gives us his unconditional love and sal-vation, as Jesus demonstrated by eating with notorious sinners in Mark 2:16-17.

Another use of the little verb "come" is Jesus' calling us to come to him. Jesus says in Matthew 11:28, "Come to me, all you who are weary and burdened, and I will give you rest." In John 7:37-38 Jesus announces, "If a man is thirsty, let him come to me and drink. Whoever believes in me, as the Scripture has said, streams of living water will flow from within him." Jesus told the rich young ruler in Mark 10:21, after a conversation about the issues of eter-nal life, to "come, follow me."

So we see that God calls us with this little verb "come."

It's almost like breathing. God exhales and comes to us and inhales and calls us to come to him.

But God has an even bigger plan. Throughout the Gospels we find that God wants to reproduce the same sort of action in us. God commands us to go to other people and call them to come to him. The Great Commission (I refer to it frequently in this book because it is the hallmark of our call as ministers) says, "go and make disciples of all nations. . . ." We are to come to all the nations and invite them to come to God.

Jesus' parable of the great banquet says very clearly that this ought to be the activity of the people of God. In this story the master tells the servant, "Go out to the roads and country lanes, and make them come in, so that my house will be full" (Luke 14:23). In another example of this "coming," John 1 tells how Philip came to Jesus and realized that he'd found the Messiah, God with skin on, the answer to all life's questions. So Philip went to Nathanael, whom many scholars believe to be his brother, with this invitation: "Come and see." From Nathanael's perspective, Philip came to him and invited him to come to God.

Thus we find the guidelines for ministry built around the little word "come." Surely this is an appropriate activity for every Christian who is serious about becoming Christlike, especially those of us whom God has called to ministry. After all, God has called us to make a life's vocation out of imitating the ministry of Jesus Christ. We have responded to God's call to come to him daily, moment by moment. We must accept the commission that God has given us to go to others and to call them to come. This is the essence of Christian life, the connecting point between God and man.

But how do we do this effectively with teenagers? It sounds good, but many of us have found that when the time comes to make that connection between teenagers and the Lord God Almighty—and somehow, by the help of the Holy Spirit, put them together—it's an overwhelming task. Peter was staggered by the cost of commitment in Matthew 19:25, where he observes, "Who then can be saved?" Surely with all of our weaknesses, laziness, hang-ups and unbelief it is impossible. But Jesus replied, "With man this is impossible, but with God all things are possible" (Matthew 19:26).

God can make those impossibilities possible if we allow him.

Counting the Cost—Preparing for Come Level Ministry

So what does it take, practically speaking, to have an effective come level (or evangelistic) ministry? We suggest you do five things before trying to launch an effective come level ministry:

1. First, come to God yourself for the passion and commitment necessary for other people to be brought to Christ;

2. Catch the goals and the visions of come level ministry;

3. Understand the various methods and types of come level ministry;

4. Recognize some of the common dangers of come level ministry; and

5. Understand some basic, practical principles for initiating a come level ministry in your given situation.

Let's take a closer look at these five vital areas.

Coming to God Yourself

First, you must come to God yourself to rekindle your passion, renew your commitment and focus your perspective. This will motivate you to do whatever it takes to reach a particular young person for Jesus Christ, to break through the barriers and walls that many—especially the most needy—build around themselves out of hurt. It is so easy for us to allow our zeal to flag. We should kneel on a daily basis and listen to the apostle Paul's encouragement to the Roman Christians: "Never be lacking in zeal, but keep your spiritual fervor, serving the Lord" (Romans 12:11). Surely that is God's word to us as we work to win young people to Christ.

But we often find ourselves in the situation I experienced not long ago. My wife and I were at Brooks Air Force Base in San Antonio, Texas, leading a family life weekend for a renewal group. After our first evening session we were having some refreshments with the group. My younger brother, who was also there, began to tell those folks about a time shortly after my conversion when the two of us went to a Dairy Queen. That particular Dairy Queen had little screen windows the employees lifted up and down as they took orders and served food. In my immaturity and youthful enthusiasm, I stuck my head through one of those windows and announced to the people in the Dairy Queen: "If you get tired of living life in the drudgery lane, full of frustration, turn to Jesus. He'll make a difference in your life. He has for me." Surprised, the people laughed and were somewhat amused by my enthusiasm.

As my brother told that story to the group in San Antonio, I felt a flush of embarrassment. I explained to those people that I'd been a football player and hadn't been a religious person. I hadn't read any books about how to be an effective witness. My early witnessing was simple, over-zealous, fanatically direct and aggressive. Later in life I learned how to be more tactful and skillful in meeting people where they are.

But I was also feeling a deeper flush of inner embarrassment because I realized that a lot of my passion and zeal to let other people know how fantastic it is to know God and how Jesus can bring joy and purpose had somehow become professionalized. I'd spent too much time in the comfort zone, basking in human praise and the status quo. That night in San Antonio, I was reminded how I must daily come to God for the grace to become uncomfortable at times so that I can reach young people for Jesus. God can help us care enough to make that second-mile effort often needed to see young persons through a crisis so that they will know we love them unconditionally, and that perhaps there's a God behind all of this business called Christianity.

How many of us find ourselves lapsing into the comfortable, status quo youth program that has Sunday school, a youth group and perhaps a Bible study with a number of young attenders? Everyone seems satisfied with our nice program, so surely we should be satisfied with it too. We allow ourselves to ignore the overwhelming majority of young people who don't know Jesus Christ in a personal way.

Our only hope of sustaining the commitment, vision and passion necessary to win youth to Christ is for us to move out of our offices, beyond our safety zones and into the world of teenagers, a world with hurt and sin. We must daily come to Jesus in our quiet times and our intercessory prayer for others. Only from that foundation will we be able to implement any of the other four suggestions for preparing for come level ministry.

Defining the Goals

After we come to God and receive the enthusiasm and vision to reach young people, we need to define what we're trying to accomplish through our come level ministry. Here are some of our goals:

1. To lead young people to a saving knowledge and relationship with Jesus Christ as Lord and Savior. Basically and simply, we want to help them come to God.

2. To make contact with inactive and unchurched young people. Reach the masses of humanity that don't know Jesus.

3. To create a positive, non-threatening atmosphere for relationships between youth workers and teens. Build a relational bridge between workers on the youth ministry team and teenagers over which the gospel of Christ and healing love can flow.

4. To help youth workers earn the right to be heard. We used to live in a society and culture in which authority dictated the right to be heard. If you were a teacher or a minister, for example, your position of authority created a platform from which you could speak. Since the rebellious 60s, however, authorities and institutions have been constantly questioned. We usually have to earn the right to be heard through genuineness and getting to know the young people. They must come to know us as trustworthy persons whose message is not phoney. In other words, our message must not be some institutional, traditional line in which we have no personal involvement or commitment. We must speak from a consistent lifestyle. Come level ministry gives us an opportunity to model that sort of lifestyle to youth.

5. To dispel the myths about Christianity, Christians and youth workers. Many myths about Christianity fill the minds of teenagers today, confusing them about the nature of genuine, biblical Christianity. For example, one striking need is to dispel the myths created by the recent publicity over scandals in certain television ministries that have strayed from the simplicity and genuineness of biblical Christianity. Another myth many youth accept is that God is a mean old man with a stick who hovers over the earth. When he sees someone having fun, he beats them with his stick, saying, "Pow, pow, pow, you'll have no more fun!" Or young people get the idea that if they commit their lives to God he'll send them to Africa and make them live in a grass hut. These perverted images of God often come from childhood. Come level ministry gives us an opportunity to try to shatter these myths and to share the power, simplicity, purity and beauty of the gospel with young people.

6. To create a conducive environment for friendships and thus relational ministry. In early adolescence, and even mid- to late-adolescence, friendships are king. If we can create positive peer pressure, we will protect young people from things that will destroy their lives and lead them to the way that gives life. One of the goals of come level ministry is to create that positive peer pressure.

Understanding the Techniques

After you clarify what you plan to accomplish, you'll need to understand some of the types of come level ministry. Basically, there are two categories of come level ministry and several ways to develop them: (1) relational come level ministry and (2) programmatic come level ministry.

Relational Come Level Ministry

There are three ways to accomplish relational come level ministry: (1) one-on-one contact between the youth worker or adult sponsors and the teenagers, (2) small group contact in which the number of people involved is small enough to be relational and not programmatic and (3) inter-youth contact, in which youth reach out to other youth and call them to come to God.

The One-on-One Approach. The one-on-one method, youth worker to youth, is based upon the principle Jesus taught in his parable about the Good Shepherd. Leaving the ninety-nine sheep who are safe and well cared for, the Good Shepherd reaches out to that one who, for some reason or another, won't or can't relate to the group (see Matthew 18:12-14). This one individual wanders away from the group, gets into great difficulty and needs help. In the one-on-one method, the youth worker focuses on the individual youth, builds a relationship with that youth and through that relational bridge ministers to that young person's needs with the goal of leading him or her to Jesus Christ.

When I think of this type of ministry, I remember a young man in our youth group in Wilmore, Kentucky. Actually, to say that he was in the group is kind of misleading. He had endured a terrible home life, including a horrible childhood relationship with his stepfather. He was abused in many ways, got in trouble with the law and didn't feel good about himself for obvious reasons. He seemed lost to any kind of healthy living.

I remember establishing contact with that young man and seeing his surprising response to the smallest overtures made in his direction. We went hunting together, and before long he was calling me to spend time with him, rather than my having to take the initiative.

One afternoon as we were driving home from Lexington, I began to talk to this young man about his relationship with God, his thoughts about Christianity and the Christian faith. His openness was beautiful as we discussed his questions about his problems and fears concerning a relationship with God. It reminded me again that we must not be satisfied with mere group evangelism. To individualize the gospel of Jesus we must have a relational come level ministry, interacting one-on-one with young people in our youth group, our community and our schools.

The Small Group Approach. The small group approach focuses on developing groups of young people, including those who have a low level of interest in a commitment to God.

I remembered one youth group that contained a cluster of young men who seemed to have no interest at all in the things of God. When they attended youth meetings, their only interests seemed to be playing games, causing trouble in the back of the room or seeing if they could slip out in the middle of the meeting and get away with it.

So I decided to invite this group to join me on Tuesday afternoons for a time of sports, hunting, swimming, bowling or eating. I was amazed to discover how enthusiastically these guys, who up until that time had shown no enthusiasm for our youth ministry, attended this meeting.

Each Tuesday we would take about five minutes after the activity to sit down and talk about God, the Scriptures and Christian living. We usually started with some theme relevant to their world. One Tuesday after basketball we discussed how sin is like missing the mark, like shooting the ball toward the goal and missing—hitting the rim, the backboard or nothing at all. I was amazed at how readily those young men entered into such conversations and seemed to gain a greater understanding of the biblical explanation of sin.

That's an example of a small group come level event, which may be built around a sport or hobby. It has a small group dynamic which enables you to know the individual needs of each person in that group.

The Youth-to-Youth Approach. I feel the most effective come level ministry is youth-to-youth. In youth-to-youth relational ministry, young people who have made a commitment to God advance to grow level programming (see chapter five). At the grow level we teach them that one of the integral activities of being a Christian is to come to God first and then to go to other people and call them to God as well. After this grow level training we begin to hold these youth accountable through our discipleship level ministry (see chapter six). We give them opportunities to reach out to peers and to report on the success or failure of their efforts in a come level ministry. Next, through our leadership training (see chapter seven), we go beyond holding youth accountable and begin to teach them different principles and methods, giving them long-term leadership development projects. At the end of the leadership training process, they conduct actual extended one-on-one come level ministry relationships with persons. So we help these young people become skillful in inviting their friends to come to God. We find that this is the most successful and effective approach to youth ministry.

I'm reminded of a young man in our leadership program for high school juniors and seniors. At one youth meeting he shared how he had invited a youth named Bill fishing. Well, everyone in that room knew that Bill wasn't interested in church or being associated with Christians. But the young man in our leadership program was a great outdoorsman and was able to meet Bill where he was. He and Bill began doing activities together and thus building a relationship. We're confident that God will be able to use that relationship to touch Bill in a significant way. Maybe he'll never come to Christ, but he's been touched by the body of Christ and has the opportunity to get to know God in a meaningful way.

Programmatic Come Level Ministry

The second type of come level ministry is programmatic. We use two methods of programmatic come level ministry. One is the regular, weekly meeting that is the port of entry into the youth group. It focuses on the goals of come level ministry in order to reach young people in the school and community. This weekly meeting gives youth an opportunity to join the group, to come to Christ and to make a change in their living.

The second method of programmatic come level ministry is a special event. It is also dedicated to the goals and purposes of come level ministry.

Out-of-the-Ordinary Weekly Youth Meetings Set the Stage. It's important to plan a variety of activities that relate to the young people of your area in your weekly meetings. Our Wilmore program has a Sunday night event that we call Breakaway. Basically, it's our denomination's youth fellowship.

In our Breakaway gatherings we try to feature an activity that is disarming, amusing, flabbergasting or even gross. For example, we might show youth a film on skiing. Another night they might hear a speaker who's a professional athlete. Someone may crawl through a window. We might play a game in which we fight with enormous pillows. We may burst balloons on each other's rear ends. We may play a game of war outside with water balloons and shaving cream.

This wide variety of events reflects the basic focus of come level ministry. We want young persons to be able to invite their friends to our youth group. These friends should be able to come to our youth group and not be confused by deep issues that don't relate to them as non-Christians. They should be able to observe people who love each other. These meetings allow youth to meet adult youth workers who can arrange opportunities for one-on-one contact and ministry.

Such meetings also help dispel myths about Christians being stuffy, having no fun and being out-of-touch with the rest of society. We want to create an environment where youth can get to know some positive peers.

We want to bring young people to Jesus through our programmatic approach. Also, if you'll remember our funnel illustration, this come level provides a weekly program around which to focus publicity and relational ministry. It is the base camp for come level ministry.

Special Events Attract New Members. One of the most effective ways to programmatically reach young people is through special events. Many youth will never come to your church for a meeting. Often they are attracted to the church and youth group through some sort of special event. Once there, they have an opportunity to come to Christ.

We use a host of special events: backpacking trips, canoe or rafting trips, outings at local amusement parks, skating, bowling. Find out what activity appeals to the youth of your area and use that effectively.

We encourage our young people to invite their friends,

especially friends who don't attend other churches and are not committed Christians.

Recently our group went on a backpacking trip. As we sat around the campfire at night, one of our youth workers began to share just what it meant to leave frustrations, failures and defeat behind and start over with Christ. A young man who had been struggling for years chose to rededicate his life to Jesus at that campfire. Since then his life has been totally transformed. Yet, he did not go on that trip because he liked church. He went because he loved backpacking.

Recognizing the Dangers

As we've seen, to prepare an effective come level ministry, we must come to God ourselves for passion and commitment. We need a clear idea of what we're trying to do. We need to know some of the different methods we can use to accomplish our goals. And we also need to recognize the inherent dangers of having a come level ministry.

Stopping at the Come Level

One of the dangers is becoming preoccupied with come level ministry and not offering anything beyond it. Recently, a friend told me about a youth leader in our denomination and his particular approach to youth ministry. This minister was able to attract large numbers of youth to churches where he served, and tremendous job opportunities were available to this man because of his success. But my friend's last word about this individual's ministry was that he offers no discipleship training. It seems that he can produce a large group of young people but not much more than that. He's not able to lead them beyond the come level.

We must beware of the danger of becoming totally immersed in the task of building our group. We want to have fun and foster a sense of fellowship and do all the things that are so important and good at the come level. But we must not stop there. We must not fail to call youth to a deep and daily commitment to God.

Losing Sight of the High Calling

Another danger is losing our evangelistic vision of come level ministry. Sometimes it is easy to concentrate on fun and games and excitement that please and tickle the needs and interests of youth while avoiding the "religious stuff" for fear of losing the young people's attention or involvement. For whatever reason, we often lose sight of the whole focus and purpose of having a youth ministry. We must remember that the come level ministry is designed to let us come to youth in unconditional love and then call them to come to God and get to know him personally as Lord and Savior.

Being Misunderstood

Another danger of come level ministry is that you'll be accused of having a shallow ministry. I am usually embarrassed and nervous when students from nearby Asbury Seminary come to observe our Breakaway on Sunday evening, as they often do each semester in conjunction with a youth ministry class. As they enter the youth meeting room, it must seem like bedlam. They see young people sitting in the back who are not interested, or who may be talking about some drug adventure or sexual exploit. Of course, we're trying to get those sorts of young people to come to our youth group so that they can get to know Christ. But I worry that the seminarians won't understand what the meeting is all about. They could conclude from this one meeting that this is the entire focus of our ministry. I'm sure some of them report to their professors that we have a shallow, pathetic and anemic youth ministry over at Wilmore United Methodist Church.

Making a Mess

Another danger of come level ministry is that you'll make messes at retreats, lock-ins and rowdy activities. Young people who don't respect themselves, don't respect God and don't respect property are going to make messes in your church. A few weeks ago, for example, someone wrote vulgar statements on our church bulletin board. I have an idea who did it, and I'm sure such a thing would never happen if we only held discipleship events or only allowed Christian youth who are deeply dedicated to God to participate in our youth ministry. But I think it's worth putting up with the messes in order to reach kids who desperately need Jesus. Nevertheless, you'll have to deal with this reality and the people in your church who won't like the occasional damage.

Playing Follow the Leader

Another danger is the temptation to imitate another person's come level programming. For example, Jorge conducted his youth ministry at Trinity Hill United Methodist Church in Lexington, Kentucky; I work in Wilmore, Kentucky, a small town only fifteen miles away geographically but at least 500 miles away culturally. If I try to do come level ministry exactly like Jorge, or vice versa, I will surely fail because young people in the two locations are not interested in the same things. They'll not be attracted to youth group, thus weakening the entire effect of come level ministry.

Losing Control

Another danger of come level ministry is the loss of control, which brings discipline and safety problems. This is always a struggle. Whenever you work with young people you don't really know, you haven't had time to gain their respect and to use that respect to motivate them to do the things you'd like them to do and refrain them from being too rowdy. Any time you gather a large group of youth, you will have some discipline problems. This is such a vital concern for most youth ministers that I have included the following separate article.

How to Get Youth to Mind Without Losing Yours!

Time after time during seminars for youth workers, youth leaders plead for insight into motivating youth to behave. I don't profess to have any easy answers. Yet, I have found that discipleship-oriented, relational ministry (see chapter nine) gives youth leaders a distinct advantage in administering discipline because it em-

phasizes earning the right to be heard (credibility and respect). This emphasis, I am convinced, is the ultimate key to successful discipline and motivation in youth ministry.

When endeavoring to gain and keep order among teens, one can use two approaches: internal or external motivation. Internal motivation seeks to effect desirable behavior through respect, loyalty and helping the youth understand the reasons for our standards. External motivation tries to effect desirable behavior through reward/punishment fear/pleasure techniques.

Both approaches are necessary. However, the youth worker's best choice is internal motivation. Unfortunately, many of us spend an inordinate amount of time screaming, pleading, threatening and bribing our youth to cooperate (all of which are external motivations). Therefore, I encourage an approach that radically and creatively moves all discipline approaches and problems toward credibility-gaining, respect-building relationships (internal discipline). In this spirit, I offer the following guidelines for providing discipline in youth ministry.

(1) Youth will much more readily listen and respond to adults they respect and love. Thus, concentrate on building personal relationships that foster credibility and loyalty.

(2) Start your relationship building with your best and worst behaved youth. Generally, the others will follow these groups.

(3) Call on youth to respect you and your leadership by clearly explaining your goals and expectations. Behavioral expectations for come level events should be very different from those for discipleship level events.

(4) Involve the youth in gaining and maintaining order. After the first year, I rarely begin or proceed in an event until the youth have quieted themselves and their unruly peers. (This approach is especially effective when youth at the discipleship and leadership training levels are in the group.)

(5) When a young person violates a standard:
a. maintain emotional control (wait before res-
ponding if necessary);
b. evaluate the offender's attitude; if it is good,
assume he or she did not intentionally mis-
behave, but rather committed a sin of poor
judgment. Make sure your expectations are
clearly explained;
c. confront troublemakers one-to-one when
possible (discussing misbehavior with three
adults to one youth can also be effective);
d. never attack youth verbally or physically;
e. offer the young person options that will
create an opportunity for relationship and ministry.
(6) When serious offenses, habitual offenses of
blatant rebellion occur, call the youth's parents.
(7) When all else fails, in consultation with parents
and authorities, conditionally revoke the youth's
privilege of attending most events. Keep your
relationship with the youth alive, however, if at
all possible.

*I share the following testimony from one church in
which I ministered to give a flesh-and-blood illustration
of how these principles work.*

*At one Sunday evening youth meeting, I noticed the
youth tossing something in the back of the room. Upon
closer inspection, I discovered it was an inflated con-
dom. I was disgusted to discover young ladies were involved in the incident.*

*As we walked to my office, I wanted to unload my
frustration and anger at their making light of two very
sacred institutions: the church and sex. Yet, somehow,
I believe the Holy Spirit tempered my legitimate but
overly negative emotional reaction with genuine agape.*

*I shared my concerns with these girls honestly and
emphatically. Then in an effort to stop this activity for
a lifetime rather than just to slow its progress at church,
I offered them the option of my calling their parents or
their meeting with me for one hour a week for four*

weeks. Miraculously, they instantly developed a great desire for counseling with their youth minister.

In our meetings we discussed self-esteem, God's view of sexuality, salvation and careers. Through our meetings, I grew to appreciate these young ladies, and I feel they grew in their respect for God and the church. Following this incident, I had little or no discipline problems with these girls. In fact, later that year, two of them came forward at an altar call to receive Christ as Savior.

Putting Come Level Ministry into Practice

Having recognized the need to guard against the dangers of come level ministry, we finally reach the point of making come level ministry work in our situation. It's one thing to talk about compassion, goals, methods and dangers, but the real question is, "How do I do it in my situation? Where do I start?" Certainly, we can't answer every question, but the following guidelines can help you launch your come level ministry.

Begin in Jerusalem

The first priority in beginning a come level ministry ought to be one-on-one ministry. You need to start where you are with young people in your church, school and community. Start in your Jerusalem. Use the list of young people in your youth group. Also, search your church's youth rolls to locate youth you haven't seen in a long time and those who have given no indication of why they haven't been coming to your group. List those young people as the focus of come level ministry and concentrate your relational ministry on them.

Next, make a plan. Pray for those people every day, or divide the list and pray for several people a day. Do whatever works for you, but begin to pray for each person.

Then take action. Don't simply pray and intend to do good things, but actually begin to make contact with those young people. A plan that has helped me move toward the young people in my group and community is to hold myself accountable every week for contacting six young people. I try to include two who either aren't Christians as far as I know, or, if they are, they aren't active in a church. These are young people I would classify as being in the come level category.

Each week the list of inactive young people grows and expands. Each Monday morning I write down from that list the two come level youth I will contact that week.

Usually, I pick up the phone and call them to schedule an appointment to get together with them after school. In some cases, I don't know the young person well enough to make a phone call, so I try to determine how I can get to know that young person. Do I know some of that person's friends? Is that person an athlete? If so, I'll attend his ball games. Does that person usually hang out in a certain parking lot, or does he or she have a job where I can drop by and make a brief contact? Designate a particular time (for me it's usually after school on Tuesdays and Thursdays) to contact that person.

Guidelines for One-on-One Ministry

Once you've made a plan of action, you can use four C's as a guideline in your one-on-one contact ministry. The C's stand for *contact, contract, convince* and *consistent.*

Make Contact. Contacting youth is one of the scariest things we do as youth ministers. When working with inactive, unchurched or unknown people, it's difficult to go in cold, make conversation and try to build relationships. But I find that most young people are hungry at the deepest level of their being for unconditional love. Most young people long to talk to someone they see as a stable adult about the things that are going on in their lives. They're in a tremendous struggle to determine their identity and sexuality, and they worry about building their future, making decisions and understanding emotions. They need someone they can trust who has gone through those experiences.

After moving beyond any initial barriers, my experience has been that most young people are very open. In fact, I have never had a young person turn down an opportunity to meet with me. That's pretty significant, considering I have worked in a county seat town in Mississippi, the inner city of Dallas and tiny Wilmore, Kentucky. I've never known a young person to consistently say no to such an invitation.

Exactly how should you initiate a contact? I find it's best to begin by asking the young person some questions. Greet them and be cordial to them. Don't smother them, but ask them what interests them. A question that I usually use is: "When you have free time to do anything you like, what do you do?" Most young persons will mention sports, watching television, a hobby or music.

Agreeing to a Contract. After several conversations, I usually try to set up a time when we could do together whatever activity interests them. Most young people are very eager to share their interests with you. This is the part of the relational ministry I call the contract.

It often goes something like this. Let's say you're contacting a person named Bill. Bill sits in the back of the youth group and doesn't have much to say. You don't know anything about him, so during the refreshment time you ask Bill, "How are you doing?" Bill grunts and mumbles. You say, "Well, Bill, how's your week gone?" But he's still not very interested in speaking. "What did you do this past week?" you ask. And he grunts again, so you let it slide and say, "Well, it's good to see you."

Then, the next time you see Bill, you ask him a series of other questions.

Eventually, Bill is either going to get so frustrated that he leaves and never comes back (which rarely happens), or he begins to open up a little bit about what's going on in his life. And from that modest beginning, you try to locate a point of interest where you and he can get together. Maybe you discover that Bill loves skateboarding and you know nothing about it. You say, "Bill, that really sounds like fun, but I've never done that before. Could we get together on Tuesday afternoon for you to teach me a little about skateboarding?" Six times out of ten, the first time you ask, they will decline your invitation. But eventually they will agree, perhaps out of consideration for you, if you tactfully keep asking. This gives you an opportunity to begin to form a relationship.

You contract for an appointment to spend an extended

time together so that the relationship can develop. This is not always a smooth process, however.

About six months ago, I took a young man out to eat pizza after calling to invite him. We spent about two hours together, and during that time this young man said maybe five words. I almost had a nervous breakdown! I asked him every question I could think of. I went to the bathroom. I played with the straw. We had long, uncomfortable periods of silence as we somehow sputtered and muttered through that contact time.

Today, however, this young man is a little bit warmer, a little bit more open. He will seek me out sometimes to wave at me or to get my attention, all because of my feeble effort to meet him and set up an appointment.

Convincing Youth that We're "For Real." Another important function of relational ministry is to convince young people that we care. Whether we're merely greeting them, smiling or making small talk, or contacting them and contracting for a meeting time, we must convince them that we love them unconditionally. We must let them know that we don't want anything from them. We're not paying attention to them just because we want them to come to our youth group, or because we want them to make a commitment to God. We must convince young people that we have an honest interest in ministering to their needs.

If you don't have this genuine love for youth, you need to go back to step one. You need to come to Jesus and allow him to renew you and create in you a concern for youth, or you should get out of youth ministry altogether. The effectiveness of relational, one-on-one contact ministry depends on convincing a person that you care unconditionally.

As God opens the door for you to do this, you also want to convince a young person that God has the same sort of love for him or her that you do—that Jesus Christ died for his sins, and he has an opportunity for a fantastic life as a committed Christian. You want to convince young people to whom you minister of the gospel's validity and relevance.

Being Consistent Counts. The last C that you want to follow in your one-on-one ministry is to be consistent. Regardless of what happens in your youth ministry and personal life, you want to consistently show love to young persons. A young person may not come to Christ or attend youth group, but if that person allows your relationship to grow and develop, you can be a redemptive presence in that person's life. We do this by being consistent in our love and ministry.

I'm reminded of a young lady I've met with on and off every week for about three years. Unfortunately, this young lady has not made a commitment to God. In fact, she seems to have grown more distant from God in the last three years. Her life has followed a downward spiral into drugs, promiscuity and a legion of sinful and self-destructive activities, so that her mental health has deteriorated with each passing year. Yet this young person has allowed our relationship to continue. She has met with me at times when she didn't really want to. At other times this young person has pursued our relationship and eagerly sought out an opportunity to get together over a cola or to take a walk.

I am convinced that through the last three years this young person has had an opportunity to experience unconditional love, to be accepted regardless of her own ability or willingness to respond. And I believe God will not only use that redemptive presence in her life in the future, but he is also using it as a stabilizing influence in her life now.

Instigating a One-on-One Ministry in Your Situation. When beginning a one-on-one relationship with a young person, remember to start where you are. Make a plan and bathe it in prayer. Contact individual youth. Contract with those youth for further meetings. Convince them of the reality of God and your genuine, unconditional love for them. And be consistent in your love and relationship with them, regardless of their response.

Guidelines for Small Group Ministry

The same principles hold true in small group relational ministry as in the one-on-one relationship. The only difference is in the small group situation. How do you produce a come level small group?

Very often, you'll find a group of young people already divided into small groups, especially during early adolescence. Youth tend to move and function in groups. It's often difficult to isolate a younger teen one-on-one because they feel uncomfortable and insecure in that situation. They're more apt to meet with you in a small group.

Because of this tendency, you can easily build small groups around activities that teens enjoy. For example, a woman on our ministry team has built a small group around visits to the mall. Junior high or teenage girls certainly enjoy going to the mall, but in our rural community it's often difficult for those who don't have a driver's license to get there. So every Tuesday afternoon this youth minister gives the teens in our church an opportunity to go to the mall.

This effort has resulted in a small come level group. She began to build a relationship with the girls and eventually invited them to come to God.

While serving in Dallas, I met a group of young men who were far from becoming Christians. They were inner-city thugs who had the reputation of being bad dudes. I knew many of them one-on-one, having spent time playing ball and going hunting and fishing with them, but we had never done much else together.

One day, I caught the group discussing God. They allowed me to enter that discussion, which had begun spontaneously. I invited them to meet with me on Tuesdays during the noon meal to discuss spiritual issues or anything else they wanted to talk about.

For the next two years, as I described in chapter one, this group called the Outlaws met each week. The opportunity for ministry among these young men was incredibly rich and exciting.

You can build small groups around hobbies, sports, interests, needs, jobs, projects or whatever you can create or discover to bring young people who are usually not interested in Jesus Christ into contact with you. This contact can lead them to God and to the church.

Getting Your Programmatic Come Level Ministry Off the Ground. Here are some practical suggestions for building a programmatic come level ministry:

■ *Bait your hook.* Find out what interests young people. Explore the "youthscape" of your particular youth group, church, community and school.

One way to do this is through interviews and surveys. It

is amazingly easy to get youth to express their opinions. Mid- and late-adolescents especially enjoy sharing their views on different matters.

You can conduct your survey through personal interviews, by eating lunch with youth at school, by distributing survey forms at youth meetings or, if you're given the chance, through the public school system or some community youth event. The survey should be designed to reveal the interests of young persons in your community.

Interview them about everything, from what they like to do with their free time, to their favorite music, to their ideas about dating. Try to get the sort of information that will help you build a solid, interesting and relevant youth program.

If you don't want to tackle anything quite as formal as a survey or if you're unable to, simply interview your young people. Whenever I enter a new church situation, I interview every young person in the youth group. I don't call it an interview, I call it "getting together" with them. I do this to take the pulse of our youth group, collectively as well as individually. This helps me learn what their interests are and what they think it would take to meet the needs of the youth in that community.

No matter how you do it, you need to get to know your young persons. Only then can you plan events that will bring young people to Jesus Christ, create a positive peer group, earn the right to be heard, present the gospel and dispel the myths many young people have about Christianity.

A friend of mine, James Loftin, is the youth minister of a church in Memphis, Tennessee. The youth he ministers to have a totally different social background than the young people to whom I minister. It would be a great mistake for me to duplicate James Loftin's come level programming in Wilmore, even though some of what I know about come level ministry I've learned from him. If I did this, chances are we would lose three-fourths of our young persons because what is relevant, interesting and meets the needs of young people in Memphis, Tennessee, is not at all what is needed in Wilmore, Kentucky. So it is vitally important to study your youth community, to find out who is interested in a commitment to God and who is not and to determine the best way to reach those persons by meeting them where they are.

■ *Build your come level program around your young people's interests.*

Target the group of people to whom you want to minister. I've already mentioned that your come level ministry ought to start with the list of inactive and unchurched youth in your own youth group.

As you move beyond this list, focus your ministry on the interests, needs and availability of young people in your community. This might mean that you need to meet on Tuesday rather than Sunday evenings, or on Saturday mornings instead of Sunday mornings. You'll do whatever it takes to make your program effective and relevant if you're serious about meeting your young people where they are with the good news of Jesus Christ.

Also, I suggest that as you build a come level program you do not require the same commitment as you would from youth in a grow level event, such as a Bible study. Structure come level events so that any young person who is willing and interested can be a part of that event without feeling trapped by a lot of confusing requirements and concepts. For example, if some of the youth who share joints at the high school and have never been exposed to the Christian faith attended our mission preparation meetings where youth kneel at the altar and earnestly pray that God would purify and strengthen them, one of two things would happen. Either the rowdy teenagers would fall to their knees, or they would be turned off, misunderstand and probably not come back. So don't require a high level of commitment at the come level. Don't involve unprepared, unchurched youth in something that they can't understand or readily be a part of.

■ *Learn to creatively publicize your event.*

Unchurched and inactive youth won't attend meetings to hear your announcements. Their parents probably aren't informing them about what's going on, and chances are that if you send them a newsletter they won't read it. You've got to use creative publicity to reach these young persons.

This could involve obtaining permission to present a

video at school. It may mean gaining permission to let a Christian rock star eat lunch in the school cafeteria to publicize the event you're hosting at your church that evening. Recently, we had a young man from the Altar Boys, a Christian Rock Band, visit our local school lunch room. He looked like somebody from outer space, but young people were drawn to him. His visit was great publicity for the Christian rock festival that was happening in our little town that weekend.

But your best approach to publicizing your program is to rely on friendships. Your young people can successfully invite their friends, who will trust that there will be a safe place for them in the group. It's disconcerting for any of us to walk into a room of seventy-five or twenty-five or even six people we don't know. We're not sure how they're going to act or what's going to happen. But if we can go with someone who is our friend and who has invited us, we're more likely to attend.

■ *Learn to use your available resources to produce an exciting, fast-moving, quality event that will meet young people where they are while still making a clear and winsome presentation of Jesus Christ and his love for them.* Let me share with you our basic format for a come level event, keeping in mind that we deviate from this format as much as we follow it.

Generally, on a Sunday night we begin with a "plaza time," the first fifteen or twenty minutes when young people are gathering. (Usually youth don't arrive all at once. It's unrealistic for you to think they're all going to be sitting there at seven o'clock or whenever your meeting starts.) Sometimes the plaza time will be like a carnival; we'll have games where youth can throw hoops, try to burst balloons with darts or throw balls to knock things down to win albums or candy. Or we may have some games going on such as volleyball, steal the bacon or parking lot hockey. This gives them something to do besides standing there and feeling uncomfortable and insecure. Plaza time also gives youth and the youth ministry team a chance to sit around and talk casually. Meanwhile, we always play contemporary Christian music to create an exciting atmosphere.

Next, we usually go right into a time of lively singing. We

encourage our young people who are committed to God to make the singing exciting and create an atmosphere of life and enthusiasm.

After our singing we move into some unexpected event— a skit or a stunt, such as calling someone to the front for a pie in the face or a contest of balancing a broom on your nose—whatever we can come up with to create an atmosphere of fun, warmth and the life that God brings to us. We might show a video that we've recorded ourselves. Perhaps we've recorded a skit at the local school that makes an amusing point about living one's life at school as though God doesn't exist. The video may show Jesus standing by as a person goes to a locker and says vulgar words.

After the unexpected event, we usually tend to get a little more serious. We sing a song that's more worshipful and slow the pace down a little bit. We may have one of our young persons share how Jesus Christ made a difference in his or her life that week.

Next we go into what we call "the rap." The rap is usually introduced by some experience. For example, we may have everybody build a human pyramid. When it gets about twenty people high, it falls to pieces. During the rap we explain how when your life is crumbling, and you can't keep your friendships, your dating life or your home life together, God can put things back together and make all things new.

We usually close our Breakaway event with refreshments.

Of course we might not do any of these specific things on a Sunday evening, but our general format usually flows in this direction. The point is, you need to use what's available to you to create a meeting where there's a sense of excitement, warmth, unpredictability, joy and a clear presentation of the gospel of Christ.

You also need to make sure that your staff people, youth sponsors, parents and pastor share the vision. You must convince them of the need for these activities and explain the goals of what you're trying to accomplish. Call on them to assist you with finances, with their time and with their help to conduct an effective come level program.

Be intentional about interacting and having fellowship with the young people who come, including the visitors and those who don't feel a part of the group. They may have come for social reasons, or maybe they were not invited but just showed up. Make sure that someone doesn't attend your come level event, stand against the wall, never get spoken to and leave. That could do more harm than good. Make sure that someone not only greets them and you talk with them, but also that your staff, youth sponsors and, most importantly, your youth take time to talk with them.

■ *Be sure to include a strategic presentation of the gospel.* Whether through drama, a skit, a video, a tape, a musician, a solo or a rap, make sure you don't allow a young person to attend your come level event and walk away without having heard the words of life.

■ *Use the interests and the resources of your church and community to develop come level special events.* If you live in a rural area, going to a city seems to draw young people. If you live in the city, wilderness and rural events seem to attract more youth.

Too often we get the impression that our special events have to be big, expensive and extravagant. Most young people are thrilled at the opportunity to just get together to do something entertaining, whether it's going to a lake, having a picnic, watching a baseball game, going to a movie or visiting an amusement park. *What you do is not as important as who's going.* If you can get your young people to invite their peers and convince their friends that everyone's going, it will be a successful event.

Guidelines for Youth-to-Youth Ministry

We have purposely left discussing strategies for implementing a youth-to-youth relational come level ministry until last. This type of come level ministry forms slowly. It takes time for young people to build a lifestyle that reaches out to other people. And yet, youth-to-youth come level ministry is the most important and effective way to reach young people in your church and your community for the Lord Jesus.

The next three chapters tell in detail how the grow level, discipleship level and leadership training level help committed youth gain a vision for ministry to the inactive and unchurched young people in your community, so we won't spend a lot of time now on that subject. But we must note here that it is impossible for you to give youth a vision and passion for reaching out to people who don't know God unless you model that vision and passion yourself. Unless relational ministry is a part of your own lifestyle, it's going to be very difficult for you to lead your youth to behave that way.

Young persons first come to our group and begin to spend time with us for a variety of reasons. As they grow in their interest in the things of God, they may come to the point where, whether gradually or in a Damascus Road type experience, they commit themselves to God. They're attracted to Christ, and they want to follow him and be everything God wants them to be. They then begin to attend youth group because of a desire to grow as Christians instead of the other reasons that we used to attract them to our come level ministry, such as our genuine, unconditional love.

When youth come because they want to grow, we need to have an effective grow level ministry that will teach them "what does the Lord require of you . . .?" (Micah 6:8). These committed youth want to know what a Christian ought to do, what God thinks about sex, what God thinks about them and other dynamics of Christian growth. We Christians who are committed to young people should offer them a ministry dedicated to Christian growth. The next chapter describes this grow level ministry which, by the way, is also based upon relationships. The personal interest does not stop when teens begin to show some commitment to the ministry.

Youth involved in this type of growth program are on their way to performing effective youth-to-youth relational ministry as they interact with their peers and draw them to come level programs.

Grow Level Ministry

Helping Young People Mature in Their Relationships with God

By Hule Goddard

The April 1987 *Reader's Digest* contained a story about twelve-year-old Jesse Morgan from Crystal Lake, Florida. The boy was snorkeling peacefully in clear Millers Creek pond when suddenly an alligator came out of nowhere and grabbed him around the head. Because of his mask and snorkel, he was able to break away with only a scalp wound. As he frantically swam away from this alligator, his mother stood on the shore screaming and pleading with her son to swim faster. The drama climaxed with the mother grasping the boy's hand and the alligator clamping down on the young man's leg. The mother dug her fingernails into her son's hands and wrists and pulled him away from this huge alligator. Her son was truly in the jaws of death, and her struggle to rescue him was literally a fight for his life.

How often do you feel as though you're involved in the same sort of battle when you try to help young people grow? It seems that the media, individual self-centeredness, school life, home life—almost our entire culture—has clasped jaws of secularism and narcissism around our kids, pulling them away from God. We frantically struggle along with the Holy Spirit to help young people grow spiritually despite all of this.

Created to Grow

Something inside all of us gives us a passion for growth. Why do we enjoy spring so much? Because we delight in seeing things come to life from the brown, dormant winter landscape. Something inside us respects and feverishly strives for growth in our physiology, our mental development and our emotional state. Jesus uses a vivid example of God's gift of creative growth in the parable of the sower (Mark 4:1-20) to appeal to this deep-seated desire. This story of seeds being planted in the earth describes our human spiritual growth. Some seeds never grow at all, some fall upon rocky soil or thorny and weedy soil and some seeds fall in good soil. Jesus' analogy helps us understand God's great desire for all of us to grow into men and women of God.

The apostle Paul makes clear the source of spiritual growth in 1 Corinthians 3:6: "I planted the seed, Apollos watered it, but God made it grow." What a relief it is to know that we are not responsible for being the ultimate source of growth. We are simply instruments of God; his ability and power cause people to grow.

Scripture shows us that God's desire and commandment to us as Christians, and especially to young people, is to grow. Ephesians 4:15 says that "we will in all things grow up into him who is the Head, that is, Christ." 1 Peter 2:2 encourages us to "Like newborn babies, crave pure spiritual milk, so that by it you may grow up in your salvation. . . ." 2 Peter 3:18 tells us to "grow in the grace and knowledge of our Lord and Savior Jesus Christ." But perhaps the most vivid picture of God's desire for and demonstration of growth is in Luke 2:52, which says the boy Jesus "grew in wisdom and stature, and in favor with God and men." So surely God's desire for all people to grow mentally, physically, socially, emotionally and spiritually should be a burden on our hearts. We should feel this as a call; indeed, it ought to be an integral part of our ministry.

The Nuts and Bolts of Christian Growth

Our funnel illustration, discussed in chapter three,

shows we must be involved in that great cycle of coming to God, realizing that God has come to us and allowing ourselves to be used to call others to come to God. After people come to God, they develop a desire to reorder their lives and to follow a lifestyle pleasing to God. We will define this as "Christian growth." Thus we ought to have a track in our ministry specifically aimed at helping young people grow.

We know that this sort of growth ought to take place and it's certainly a desire, as Scripture tells us, of the almighty God. But how do we do it? How can we effectively nurture this sort of growth in our young people? How can we devise a track of growth programming in our youth department—whether we have six youth in a small rural church or 600 in a suburban or inner-city church? How can we help our young people, who are willing to "obey everything I have commanded you," (as Jesus instructed in the Great Commission in Matthew 28:20) to grow?

To effectively construct a grow level ministry, you need to understand and implement five concepts. First, continue to grow in Christ yourself. Second, clarify and specify your goals of what you're trying to accomplish through your grow level ministry. Third, understand the various types of grow level ministry approaches. Fourth, recognize the difficulties inherent in grow level ministry, both relational and programmatic. And fifth, learn some practical techniques for implementing a grow level program in your church.

Grow in Christ Yourself

I often take young people to the San Luis Valley in Colorado to hike in the Sangre de Cristo Mountains. This hike begins at the Great Sand Dunes National Monument, which is a desert about 8,000 feet high. This particular area boasts of offering, from that desert floor to the mountain peak, all the different climates of the earth—desert, mountain, valley, north wood spruce and conifer environs, then tundra above the tree line like that in the Arctic Circle.

As we hike through those environments with the young people, I'm reminded of the different growth levels in our lives. Often, youth ministers or pastors try to lead people to the mountain peaks, to high experiences of growth and development in Christ, while they themselves live in the desert. No wonder both youth and youth ministers often experience burnout and frustration.

As I visit churches across the nation, I almost always find that the youth minister's personal spiritual life is a microcosm of his or her youth group's spiritual status. Of course, God is not dependent on our spiritual growth for what he does in our youth group, but it's difficult for him to move our young people into spiritual vitality when we're speaking to them from the desert. If we're so busy doing things for God that we don't have time for our own personal spiritual development, then our own young people will often suffer.

In 1 Timothy 3, the apostle Paul lists the requirements for overseers or ministers. Verse 3:2 tells us one requirement is being able to teach. This no doubt means one needs some natural abilities, but I also think Paul means being able to teach in the sense of having experience, growth and ongoing vitality. The apostle also mentions that overseers should not be recent converts (3:6). I think one of the reasons for this is because a minister needs to be a person who has experienced Christian growth and is well on his or her way toward Christian maturity. Certainly, then, we overseers and youth ministers should be involved in personal spiritual growth on a daily basis ourselves. (We'll discuss this in depth in chapter nine.)

What specifically does this mean? We ought to be involved on a daily, weekly and extended basis—perhaps a weekend or a week's conference—in personal growth activities. We ought to practice rigorous Bible study and participate in fellowship and prayer groups. We should regularly attend worship service, not because it's a job requirement, but because it's a vital part of our growth in Jesus Christ.

Most importantly, perhaps, we ought to have a learner's attitude. We should humble ourselves and realize that we don't know it all and haven't accomplished it all. We know this is true, but sometimes we feel the pressure, as we stand before young people, to maintain a facade of spiritual superiority. But God can most effectively help us grow when we humble ourselves and admit to him (and to ourselves and other people) that we have many growing edges, that we too need and are hungry to grow.

Clarify the Goals of Grow Level Ministry

In addition to continuing to grow spiritually yourself, you need to have a clear idea of what you're trying to accomplish in grow level ministry.

Understanding Our Most Important Goal

Our first and probably foremost goal in grow level ministry is to motivate, nurture and foster growth in young people's personal relationships with Jesus Christ.

I often accompany our youth leadership team to preach revivals. Often during the revival we extend a challenge for Christian discipleship, to commit one's life to Jesus Christ as Lord and Savior. Very often young people will respond. One of the thrills of youth ministry is seeing the openness and willingness of young people to come forward and make those sorts of decisions. Of course, sometimes emotional stirrings and immaturities are responsible for these conclusions, but I'm convinced that a significant number of them are genuine, life-long decisions to follow Christ.

I'm elated when young people stand and say "Jesus is Lord of my life and I want to commit my whole life to him, to turn from all I know to be wrong and self-centered and to seek what is God-centered and right, and God will help me make it." But even though I'm excited about statements like that, there's almost a sadness in my heart as I realize the tremendous struggle awaiting each of these youth as they begin the total re-orientation of life that God wants to bring about. They will face many pains, conflicts and confusions. Somewhere, somehow their youth ministers, their local churches or caring adults need to help these young people grow.

This is the major burden of grow level ministry. Every church in the body of Christ should have a grow level ministry for people who commit themselves and desire to grow toward Christian maturity. Surely this is a goal that will stir your passion. If it doesn't, you need to return to the first concept until you can get excited about helping others grow.

Helping Today's Youth Understand God's Ways

Another goal of grow level ministry is to help young people gain God's perspective on the critical issues of their lives. What is God's perspective on salvation? How is one saved? How does one grow spiritually? How does one obtain the assurance of salvation? What does God think about you as a person? What are God's teachings on friendship, dating, sexuality, conflict management, cheating at school, sports and every important area in young persons' lives? One of the goals of grow level ministry is to help youth understand God's ways as revealed to us in the Scriptures.

Lawrence Kolberg, a leading authority on moral development, tells us that it is generally during the teen years that one of the significant, final steps in moral development takes place, "formal operation." This is when a young person stops being motivated to act morally because an authority will punish wrong action or praise right action, and he or she begins to make moral decisions because of an inward motivation, a realization that moral behavior is best for mankind as a whole. Teenagers are very idealistic as they work out their visions of what is right for mankind, what is right for them and what is right in God's eyes. You'll find young people are very interested in what God thinks about these areas of life and growth.

Combatting Spiritual Ignorance

Another goal of grow level ministry is to familiarize young people with the great themes of the Word of God. Spiritual and scriptural ignorance abounds among mainline denomination youth. This very serious problem reminds me of Hosea 4:6 where God laments that "my people are destroyed from lack of knowledge." Many of our young people are illiterate in the very words of God—the Bible. We want our young people to learn about physics, chemistry and calculus, but they remain ignorant about the issues of life and death. The great tenets of God's Word—God's love, man's sinfulness, repentance, faith, grace, justification, sanctification—are words that we might not use as we try to teach young people. But certainly these words identify concepts that are important for young people to understand.

Piaget, one of the leading developmental psychologists of the last fifty years, tells us that the early teen years are a time of transition from the concrete thinking of childhood to the adult ability to understand more abstract concepts. Principles taught in the word of God are in many ways much more abstract than concrete. You'll find that young people have a great interest in these sorts of things. At times, they have a deep understanding of some of the most profound mysteries of the Scriptures, if we only give them the opportunity to explore them. Young people are fascinated by such discussions, if they are conducted in a creative and relevant way.

Experiencing the Body of Christ

Another goal we ought to have for our grow level ministry is to help youth define and experience the body of Christ—to discover the help that the church gives as we grow up in every aspect into Christ. Hebrews 10:24 urges us to "spur one another on toward love and good deeds." So we want to foster *koinonia* (the Greek word for fellowship) within the youth group. I find as I work with young people who are hungry to grow that this dimension of creating a Christian sub-culture (positive peers) is a most vital and dynamic ingredient.

Not long ago I talked with a young man who had recently recommitted his life to Christ. As we sat at breakfast, I shared with him how there are three things that one must do to grow as a Christian. I explained to him how I couldn't guarantee that he would make it as a Christian if he did them, but that I could guarantee that if he *didn't* incorporate these three principles into his life, he would most likely fail at being a vital Christian.

The first principle is to communicate with God. The second is to have intimate friends who are committed Christians. Number three is to become involved in a small group of people who love you, can pray with you and with whom you can share your faults, defeats and victories (*koinonia*).

Such groups are crucial to teenagers' spiritual survival. If we can surround young people with supportive, motivating friends, we will have done much to insure for them a rich and long-term Christian experience. So we want, as a part of grow level ministry, to foster and initiate that sort of friendship and *koinonia* among young people in our youth groups.

Helping Youth Hear the High Call

One important goal of grow level ministry is to establish a biblical call to excellence, heroism and *agape* love among our young people.

In our age of mediocrity, most young people are only challenged in, perhaps, the arenas of education and sports. Seldom are they challenged to heroically give of themselves in service to other people—to sacrifice, whatever the cost may be, for the good of others.

We want to help youth to develop their ideal selves. Part of adolescent development is understanding who you are, building some primal convictions, determining some sort of self-esteem. But another part of the burden of healthy development is to understand and formulate the ideal self: Who do I want to be? Our grow level ministry ought to help young people construct an image of an ideal self that is committed to excellence to the glory of God, to heroic actions in the service of God and others and to unconditional support of other persons' higher good—*agape* love. If we accomplish this task, we will raise up a generation of young people who will make a difference in a world desperately in need of such excellence and character.

Understanding Grow Level Styles

In addition to growing yourself and clarifying what you are trying to accomplish in grow level ministry, you need to understand the various approaches to grow level ministry. Again, as with the come level, there are two categories of grow level ministry: the relational and the programmatic.

Relational Grow Level Ministry

Relational grow level ministry is very similar to relational come level ministry. Here we find the one-to-one relationship, (the youth worker or adult sponsor-to-youth) and the small group dynamic. We also use the youth-to-youth approach in which youth reach out to each other to help one another grow closer to Christ.

In our programmatic grow level ministry we can never, no matter how hard we try in our Bible studies, Sunday schools and youth retreats, specifically meet each youth's needs, rhythms and interests. Therefore, we must develop and emphasize a relational, incarnational approach to grow level ministry. Through **one-to-one contact with youth**— eating lunch together, then interviewing, playing ball or going to the mall—we can discover where their growing edges are—what interests or excites them, where they are failing or feeling frustrated. Through opening the Scripture and informal sharing from our own experiences, we can encourage them and help them grow.

Also, we might find **small groups** of youth who have a particular interest or urgent need in their lives. We can use that need or interest as an opportunity to help them grow. This relational approach is not generic; we aren't just selecting a topic that we feel is important and trusting God to use it in people's lives, no matter where they are.

An example of this type of small group, relational grow level ministry occurred last fall. I discovered among several senior high guys a real struggle to understand how to discern God's will and to make wise decisions in the "big five" choices of their lives. I reminded them how in the next four to ten years they would make five decisions that would affect the rest of their lives: (1) where to attend college, (2) what to major in in college, (3) what vocation to pursue, (4) whom to marry and (5) where to live their lives.

We met on a weekly basis to study some principles of guidance from the Scripture. We explored their interests and discussed ways to make wise decisions and avoid unwise choices in these vital areas of life. We built a wonderful small growth group around these five decisions.

Youth-to-youth relational ministry challenges young people, after just a little nourishment and encouragement, to get involved in helping their peers grow. You'll find that youth will readily take responsibility for their brothers and sisters in Christ.

Recently a young man in our group was struggling in his commitment to God. On three occasions, his friends in our youth group called me to alert me to the fact that he was very discouraged that day and might falter in his commitment. They pleaded with me to pray with them and to advise them on ways to help their friend. They even asked me to visit this young man. This is the sort of growth dynamic that we can create in our youth group. Concern and commitment to each other's growth will encourage young people's own individual growth in Christ.

Programmatic Grow Level Ministry

A programmatic approach is also essential to grow level ministry. Most times I favor the relational approach without apology. But that doesn't lessen the importance of our programs. We must have effective programs to provide a context for any sort of ministry. Our programs are to youth ministry what the skeleton is to our bodies. Relational ministry is to our youth program what our vital organs, skin and ligaments are to our bodies. One cannot live without the other.

Our programmatic approach to grow level ministry ought to have two phases: a weekly or regular meeting, much as in the come level, and special events.

The Weekly Grow Level Gathering. We want to make sure that sometime during the week we hold an event dedicated to Christian growth.

In our particular ministry, our major weekly grow level event is our Wednesday night Bible study, which we call Cornerstone. In your situation it may be better to meet at another time or use Sunday school for this event. (Sunday school is a given for all of us. Churches of ten or ten thousand members will have a Sunday school. The dynamic of Sunday school is unique to itself. It's somewhat a come level event, somewhat a grow level event and in some churches even a discipleship event.)

At this event, we divide the youth group into age groups that are conducive to mutual understanding. It's very difficult to accomplish many growth goals when seventh graders are thrown together with twelfth graders. (In some situations, you may not have the option of separating junior and senior high youth, but you certainly can minister to individual needs in a relational way.) We try to divide our groups along the lines of age, understanding and maturity.

During Cornerstone we study what the Scripture has to say about the relevant issues of young people's lives. It is, unapologetically, a time for serious learning, discussion and involvement with the Word of God. We make no bones about it; if a young person is not coming to Cornerstone for that purpose and is distracting others from the purpose of the meeting, we try to discipline him or her. Eventually, we may ask disrupters to leave.

Another part of our weekly program is small growth groups. We divide youth into small groups and give them opportunities to study the Bible together, serve God together and do service projects. This uses the small group dynamics we mentioned when describing relational ministry, but it is programmed and organized, with well-planned topics for study and discussion.

The Grow Level Special Event. Whether you have special events once a month or once a year, you ought to have special events focused on the grow level. Though you certainly welcome anyone to this event—whether Christian or non-Christian—the event's main objective is to help young people nurture their relationships with God and to grow in some dimension.

One of our major grow level special events each year is "Rise or Fall," a retreat we attend in northern Kentucky along with ten other United Methodist churches. The weekend is designed to inspire, through the general sessions, new and stronger commitments to God. It also features seminars, the basic bread and butter of the grow level event, that relate to specific areas of a young person's life. These seminars try to communicate a biblical, relevant perspective that will help young people grow in their walks with Jesus.

Another reason for these large retreats is to remind young people that they're not alone. The body of Christ doesn't just reside in their youth group, but in young people who are trying to grow in Christ all around their county, state and nation. Such retreats display the strength of the body of Christ to young people in a powerful way. These retreats are especially helpful to the churches with limited numbers and resources.

Spiritual life retreats can be structured around a topic— dating, self-image or friendships—and planned around that particular theme. This past year we converted our ski trip, which is normally a come level event, into a grow level event. We publicized it as that and held several sessions that focused on vital aspects of young people's struggles and conflicts and how God could help them in a powerful way. This retreat was very successful.

Recognizing Grow Level Dangers

To develop a strong, effective grow level ministry, you should understand some of the difficulties you will encounter. The first difficulty concerns the teaching methods employed in grow level ministry. So often the easy and only road that many of us know in presenting a lesson is lecturing. Unfortunately the lecture is the least effective method of teaching. Instead, we ought to be involved in discussion, experiential learning and small group learning activities.

Another significant problem in grow level ministry is that as you gather around the Scripture and focus on a more dedicated walk with Christ, your numbers become smaller. Remember, the funnel is larger at the top, so more youth will attend your come level events. Fewer people attend as succeeding funnel ministries become a little more serious. If your youth group usually numbers 100 to 150, but only fifty to seventy are attracted to grow level events, that's not too much of a blow. But if you have six to eight in your youth group and only two attend your grow level event, you can become discouraged.

During my ministry in Mississippi, I once invited a friend to visit. While he was there, I arranged for him to lead our youth Bible study. On Wednesday night he arrived with his guitar, having spent much time preparing his lesson. I assured him that several people would be there. I'll never forget the embarrassment and discouragement I felt when only two people attended Bible study that night. I was tempted to stop trying to do anything serious and growth-oriented, but I'm glad the Lord encouraged me to press on in that direction.

Another difficulty of grow level ministry is that we often feel our teaching is completed when the lesson is well presented and the youth listen, or we think we are surely successful when lively discussion of biblical truth occurred. However, Christian growth doesn't come by talk. The apostle Paul states in 1 Corinthians 4:20 that "the kingdom of God is not a matter of talk but of power." Too often we become comfortable with just teaching God's Word rather than challenging young people to incorporate it into their lives at home and school.

Another major problem found in Bible studies, spiritual life retreats and teaching situations such as Sunday school is that disinterested young people have a tendency to distract those who are interested. This is a problem because there's no accurate way to identify disinterested young people. On any given week, any young person can be disinterested or distracted. Sometimes, the whole group—no matter how hard you try—will not get serious. In these situations, we have to deal with the disrupters in love and charity. At times we have to be decisive and remove the problem youth from our Bible study. The advice in "How to Get Youth to Mind Without Losing Yours," the article in chapter four which describes discipline in youth ministry, can help you handle these situations.

Another danger we encounter as we try to help our young people grow in their relationships with others in their youth group, the body of Christ and their community is the tendency we all have to be selfish in our friendships and to develop feelings of superiority. Insecure adolescents often form cliques as they try to develop friendships. Jealousy and unwillingness to let other people become a part of their group of friends are common. Consistent disunity is an obstacle we must surmount in grow level ministry as we work to acquaint young people with the responsibility of their relationship with other members in the body of Christ.

Principles of Relational Ministry Specific to Grow Level

Most of the general principles of relational ministry are the same on all levels of ministry—whether come, grow, discipleship or leadership training. But I've discovered some significant differences when doing relational ministry on the grow level.

Get Them While They're Hot. The first principle is in contacting the youth. Unfortunately, young people rarely ever grow spiritually, or in any other way, at a steady pace. Often their spiritual growth rises and falls with the emotional and physical upheavals of this time of life. As they experience puberty and struggle with adult issues for the first time, their spiritual, emotional and physical lives consist of mountaintop peaks, small plateaus and deep valleys. Young people's ability to grow comes in seasons. As much as possible, we need to stay in touch with those seasons.

One telltale sign of a good season for growth is a young person's responsiveness at a Bible study. Also, any time a young person comes to the altar to make a commitment to God can certainly be an indication of excitement about spiritual growth. We need to contact these young people quickly while they're interested so we can help them in their individual situations. Immediate follow-up on any commitment or expressed interest is important.

Agreeing to a Contract. We also need to **contract** with interested young people to meet for three to four weeks to get all the mileage possible out of any commitment.

I remember a young man I met with every two weeks during the nine-month school year. He was not really interested in growing, and this was a come level contract. He went to camp that summer, however, where his interest in becoming a committed Christian rose to an all-time high. When he returned from camp, I quickly contacted him, and we contracted to meet four times a week for four weeks. This might seem like a bit much, but during that time he made great strides that enabled him to avoid the depths of problems and conflicts he had experienced the previous year.

We need to contract to get together for a specific time, place and duration. We also need some feedback about their needs, interests and struggles.

Be Considerate of Individual Needs. In grow level ministry, we want to console, counsel and teach young people. To accomplish this, we must focus our efforts on the hot issues of their lives. What interests them? Do they want to study the book of Revelation? Although you may not think Revelation is as relevant to their lives as Colossians or Romans, do what they're interested in and relate it to their personal situations. Find where they're hurting and center your encouragement, teaching and counseling there.

We need to be considerate in relational ministry on any level, but especially on the grow level because it tends to be seasonal. A young person's spiritual growth spurt may last for four weeks, four months or even a whole year, but we need to give that individual some space when he or she needs it. Young people have subtle but very clear ways of letting us know when they are tired of meeting or when they're not really interested in talking. We need to be considerate and back off at those times.

A recent series of meetings I had with a young lady came to the point where all we discussed were surface matters, whom she was dating that week and her interests at school. We really hadn't talked about anything of growth importance for about a month, so I mentioned that I sensed she needed some time to herself. Our meetings had run their course, and we ceased that contact time for a while. Amazingly, this kind of sensitivity can be a helpful aspect of our relational ministry.

Going the Distance. On the other hand, we need to be committed to go the distance with youth who need our support and guidance. This means we will meet as long as needed, be as faithful as needed and will take the time necessary in these relationships to help the young person grow into maturity.

Discover Needs To Build on Your Weekly Event. The youth program weekly event dedicated to Christian growth is the hub of grow level ministry. On it, we build our relational ministry, publicize our special grow level events and conduct our ongoing grow level ministry. But for this sort of grow level program to be effective, we need to discover the felt and real needs within our youth groups. (We mentioned some of the ways to do this in chapter four.) Whether you determine needs through interviewing or surveying your youth, or through reading youth ministry materials as you're doing now, I encourage you to read books about adolescent development such as David Elkind's *All Grown*

Up and No Place to Go and Ron Koteskey's *Understanding Adolescence*. Many books available at your Christian book store or library can help you understand young people and their needs.

Publicize—Creatively. To establish an effective grow level program, you must also adequately and accurately publicize your grow level weekly event at your come level events. For example, when you organize an exciting come level event to which young people are bringing their friends, at some point during that event you or a young person (or a creative balloon, flash on a screen, bulletin board, video or slide show) should present what you're trying to do in your Wednesday night Bible study or your Sunday school series. Emphasize that anyone is welcome to this event, but that the group is dedicated to Christian growth, getting to know each other as the body of Christ and developing committed relationships. All participants should understand that this is not a play event and that there is a difference between your youth fellowship (or whatever your come level event is called) and your grow level event. Make a clear, winsome, accurate presentation of what your grow level event is and what it involves.

Know Where You're Going. Another crucial ingredient in an effective grow level program is knowing what your goals are. You will want to cover relevant concerns and what God says about these issues in a young person's life.

I usually begin by exploring salvation, self-esteem, primal convictions ("what you believe"), friendships, dating, sexuality, sports, academics, social life and other pertinent topics in our grow level event. We also study the great themes of the Word of God that young people need to understand clearly and accurately for growth to occur. Generally, those are salvation, assurance of salvation, Jesus Christ as central in the New Testament, faith, repentance, justification, fellowship, witnessing, sanctification and Christian growth.

Create a Curriculum to Meet Your Goals—Not Vice Versa. After you know specifically what you want to teach your young people, you are ready to build your curriculum. Take your list of what you want to teach your young people during any given semester or series and scour catalogs or your Christian book store. Find curriculum that fits your goals rather than fitting your program to what's cheap or on sale. Although I'm not condemning those methods (I'm sure God can use them), I find it's much more effective to call the shots and to locate the material myself. I also enjoy creating my own material to fit the goals and focus of my ministry.

Understand the Learning Process. When establishing a grow level program, you need a basic understanding of the learning process. Many of us want to teach the most important issues of life—relationships with God, family, self and others—and yet we don't want to avail ourselves of the information used by experienced teachers all over America to communicate important, but much lesser, subjects. It behooves us all—interested adults, youth ministers and anyone involved in grow level ministry—to understand the basic learning process. Attend seminars, study education text books, etc., to increase your knowledge of how teens learn best.

Hold Young People's Attention. In your grow level program you must be able to hold young people's attention. One of the most painful and appalling examples of someone ignoring the need to stay in touch with the attention of the learners occurred when I was at Tyler Street United Methodist Church. One evening our district superintendent came to speak. As he was preaching his sermon, a lady collapsed in the pew. Being the only minister in the congregation (our other ministers were up on the platform) I ran to see what I could do for her. A nurse said we should call an ambulance, and I proceeded to do so. We waited and soon the ambulance pulled up. Meanwhile, the district superintendent had yet to stop preaching. The paramedics strode down the aisle, the light flashed through the church windows and the siren blared. One side of the congregation was standing up and looking to see what the paramedics were doing with their stretcher and life support equipment. Still, the D.S. continued to preach. "And Jesus called us to love other people," he exhorted. He never stopped during the entire ordeal. Not one person in that sanctuary was even aware that he was in the pulpit, yet he was finishing his sermon. He was delivering what he had prepared for the people, whether they were paying attention or not. Sometimes we teach Bible study in the same got-to-get-it-done fashion. Remember, no matter what we do, we won't be effective if we don't catch and hold the young person's attention.

But exactly how do we do this? Here are a few suggestions.

■ **Use object lessons and examples from real life to illustrate what you're talking about.** For example, one Sunday a preacher was speaking on the two sides of the nature of God, one side being love, mercy and forgiveness, and the other side being justice and wrath. He held a huge Buffalo nickel about two feet in diameter in his hand and flipped it back and forth as he talked about the two sides of the coin. That concrete example made his talk much more powerful.

Real life illustrations are another way to pique interest. Tell how someone experienced the truth and the feelings they had. Such stories should be vivid and full of emotion, action and adventure. Interesting anecdotes can focus your young person's full attention on what you have to say.

■ **Use relevant case studies**. If a young person doesn't perceive what you say as relevant to his or her life, he or she will not pay attention. We've got to convince our young people that what we are doing is so life-related, so important that only a fool would ignore these studies of God's Word.

Case studies help get this message across. Have an older person tell how a biblical truth was relevant in his or her life situation. A Christian young person can stand up and testify how God's Word is relevant in his or her life. Share examples from your own life, show a film, watch a short video . . . do anything you can to bring the particular topic or Scripture you're presenting to life.

■ **Have a clear, simple and powerfully-organized message**. You can organize a message to young people in many ways. One helpful structure in arranging the various aspects of your message is to use *preview, Scripture view, the "me" view* and *review.*

In the preview, help your audience see and feel the message and how it relates to their lives. In the Scripture view, make it clear that this is a message from Scripture. In the "me" view, help your listeners understand how Scripture applies to their lives. And in the review, summarize what was said and challenge them to action.

Our presentations must be well-organized, but they shouldn't be complex or overly in-depth. Aim for simple, powerful scriptural messages that involve and engage your young people. As mentioned earlier in this chapter, we should not overuse the lecture. Frequently involve the youth in discussions of issues, problems and confusions that a biblical approach might engender.

When it is time to present the basic Scripture view portion of the Bible study, try doing so by using small groups or have youth involve themselves in an experiential way by drawing the message out of the Scripture themselves.

■ **Observe the proper time zone**. Though rare exceptions exist, young people are seldom able to give their full attention to a Bible study, preaching or teaching session for more than twenty minutes. Try to make the meat of your Bible studies or grow level event twenty to thirty minutes long. You may want to fill the early portions of your Bible study with singing, announcements, group sharing or someone singing a special song. You can do many things to prepare young people for the study portion of your grow level event.

■ **Incorporate experiential learning in your teaching/training**. In this approach, the young person actually experiences the truth being taught. He or she comes face-to-face with the message through some sort of creative activity during or preceding the Bible study.

I often use experiential learning at stress camps and on back-packing trips. Once during a rock climb the young people experienced great fear and intimidation. Immediately following that experience, we had a discussion time and Bible study about how God helps us overcome our fears and accomplish tasks that seem too great for us. At that moment, since the youth had just experienced those emotions, their attention was riveted to God's Word and the help he has to offer.

A more down-to-earth example of experiential learning that can be used on a weekly basis is a technique I used a couple of years ago when doing a Bible study on the basic tenets of our faith. I asked a young woman whom I knew (but no one else in the youth group knew) to visit our youth group. This individual played the part of a person with some deep questions about faith. She explained that she was a high school student in town for the President's weekend at the local Christian college. She said she had asked some questions in class (high school students were allowed to attend classes held during the special weekend), and the Christians there hadn't given any really good answers. The youth in my grow level group were curious to know what questions she had asked.

"How do you know there is a God?" was her first question. I turned that over to our youth, who at that moment experienced a very real encounter with that question from a person they thought was in deep need. They began to struggle and come up with some answers. I also offered the visitor some answers I had prepared from reading various theologians, scientists, philosophers and others who have given helpful insights into how we know there is a God. The young people seemed to feed on every word I said.

The girl asked another question: "How do you know Jesus is the Son of God?" Again, I let our young people respond. Some of their ideas were quite good. Then I shared with her again from some apologetic material.

Next, she asked, "Well, how do you know the Bible is the Word of God and not any more inspired than Tolstoy?" And our young people tried to answer that question.

When that Bible study was over, our young people were aglow, buzzing with excitement about the things they had learned from that experience. It didn't seem to bother them when I told them afterwards that it was a staged experience.

The more such experiential learning exercises you incorporate into your Bible study lessons, the more you will help your young people learn about the Lord Jesus Christ and what his Word has to say.

Building *Koinonia*

Implementing a grow level program also involves building unity and genuine fellowship (*koinonia*) within the group. We should strive to build in the lives of our teens a commitment to the body of Christ by (1) understanding the goals and processes of interpersonal relationships; (2) providing activities conducive to healthy relationship building; (3) teaching the biblical imperative for unity and fellowship; and (4) establishing small groups and covenant partners.

Understanding Personal Relationships. The most practical and useful explanation of the goals and processes of building unity and fellowship are contained in Lymon Coleman's serendipity series. By using a simple baseball diamond, Colman helps us understand essential building blocks of interpersonal relationships. These include: first base (history giving, or telling your story), second base (awareness and affirmation of gifts and temperament), third base (sharing needs and goal setting), and home base (*koinonia*, indepth understanding and ministry to one another). I strongly encourage a serious youth worker to become a student of group dynamics, interpersonal communication and social sciences (i.e. sociology, anthropology.

Activities by which to Build Relationships. You can facilitate relationships by providing fun, people-oriented activities in your weekly or special grow level events. These activities should help people interact with each other.

What kind of activities are best for building fellowship? Consider the difference between a cookout or a softball game and going to a movie or a video parlor.

On one hand, at the cookout people interact with each other. They discuss cooking, talk about what they like or don't like on their hamburgers and discuss what they did last week. They sit around joking and interacting as they wait for food to cook. The softball game gives youth a chance to interact as a team, celebrate each other's gifts and commiserate over calamities. These outings provide opportunities to be together and have a relational experience. They foster fellowship/*koinonia*.

On the other hand, going to a movie, where everyone sits in a row looking at a screen, gives little opportunity to talk, respond or share things with each other. At the video game arcade, everyone is engrossed in his or her screen and its fantasy world of shooting, driving and jumping. This also allows much less interaction.

Teaching that Unity is a Biblical Imperative. You can also build a group consciousness through Bible studies, sermons and raps.

Scriptures you could explore to accomplish this unity include John 17, where Jesus, in his high priestly prayer, asked that we would be "brought to complete unity to let the world know that you sent me and have loved them even as you have loved me" (John 17:23). In John 13:35, Jesus said that all people "will know that you are my disciples if you love one another." In Ephesians 4:15-16, Paul writes that Christian growth and maturity come as each individual part of the body grows and functions in its particular role.

When our teenagers realize that unity and fellowship are vitally important to God, they will more likely view commitment to youth group as an imperative, not just a nice idea.

Small Groups Foster Unity. Small groups also help build unity and genuine fellowship. Break into small groups often at your come level events, Bible studies, Sunday school, picnics and softball games. Small groups give young people a chance to talk and share their opinions and themselves. We would hope that before long, they will share that *koinonia* commitment that we want to achieve in our young people and our youth groups.

Also encourage the formation of covenant partners. In a covenant partnership, two young people agree to pray together and share together in a one-on-one or small group situation.

Be Patient. Be realistically patient about building unity and genuine fellowship. It's a dynamic process that only the Holy Spirit can bring about—only God is able to blend people from different backgrounds into a fellowship with genuine commitment, unconditional love and unity. This unity involves sharing experiences—laughing, crying, playing and working together. *Koinonia* takes time to develop with adolescents. The social and emotional upheaval and insecurity of adolescence makes it difficult for them to maintain deep and committed friendships over the long haul.

Realize that *koinonia* will rise and fall from time to time in a youth group. The seniors graduate and the new seventh graders come in, making fellowship something we'll always be striving for. We'll always be struggling to help young people who feel left out become a part of the group, and those who feel a part of the group to open up to other people. It's an ongoing work of God's Spirit and should be an ongoing part of your grow level ministry, your discipleship level ministry and your leadership training process.

Discipleship Level—The Next Step

As we help our young people grow and they begin to understand what God requires of them, they also begin to feel tension between what they know God wants them to do and the relationship they know they ought to have with people in the body of Christ. There's also tension over who they really are, how they live at home and what they really feel toward other people. They know they ought to reach out to people in the world and be involved in God's rhythm of coming to him and going to others. They will need to decide how to act on that knowledge.

This tension lays the foundation for discipleship ministry. Discipleship ministry focuses on helping young people bridge that gap between what they know and what they do, between who they know they ought to be and who they really are. In chapter six we'll discuss ways to effectively and consistently help young people in the adventure of discipleship with the Lord Jesus Christ.

6 *Disciple Level Ministry*

Teaching Youth to Apply Biblical Principles to Everyday Life

By Hule Goddard

What is "discipleship"? The Greek word *metheo* is defined: to be a disciple, to follow a teacher's precepts and instructions. The working definition I've developed through years of youth ministry is: the process of helping young people bridge the gap between their knowledge and their actions, between their ideal selves and their real selves.

During my first year as a Christian, many of my friends— those who were discipling me—told me I ought to share the gospel with other people. I found it exciting to share my experiences. If I "led someone to Christ," everyone was thrilled. It was difficult, but I was convinced that it was the thing to do.

I shared the gospel with numerous people and lead twenty-two individuals to pray the "sinner's prayer" during my first year in Christ. However, because of my fanaticism and confrontational style of evangelism, some immature decisions were made. As I looked back over that first year, not one of those twenty-two people I prayed with was still walking with Christ. I asked myself, "What's wrong here?" I had prayed with twenty-two people who said they would turn from their old ways to God's ways. And yet not one of them had really done it! The frustration I felt helped me understand the need for discipleship.

Six years later, during my first six months at Tyler Street

United Methodist Church in Dallas, Texas, we held a spiritual emphasis week. I'll never forget how powerfully God's Spirit moved during this week. Margaret Brabon, a missionary to South America, shared simple stories about what God had done in her life on the mission field. When the invitation was given, nearly everyone in the chapel responded. People repented, asked forgiveness of one another, made commitments to life-long service and confessed sins. This went on day after day, all day long. A new spirit filled the church, and I felt like my problems were solved. From now on, I thought, my ministry is going to surge ahead from this point to even greater glory.

But two weeks after the special week, I couldn't see any difference in the church. Oh yes, some youths' lives were permanently changed, but they were precious and few. I began to ask myself some serious questions about the need for discipleship.

Not long after that, we had another opportunity for spiritual renewal at the church. I announced that this time everyone who came forward at the invitation would also commit himself to participate in six weeks of discipleship training (meeting with someone one-on-one to reinforce his decision with Bible study, prayer, counseling and teaching). I later read that John Wesley said he would not strike once where he could not strike twice. This is what we had done by giving that altar call. Not only were we giving the young people one chance to come to God, but we were also offering many more opportunities after that for counseling and encouragement.

Seventy-four young people responded to this special invitation. They prayed, made commitments to God or renewed previous commitments to God. Before they left the altar, they agreed to attend the six weeks of discipleship training. Our ministry team followed up on each youth's decision, and what a rich, reckless and exhausting time it was. God honored these young people's coming week after week. They repeated the "yes" they had said at the altar with a "yes" each week.

Six weeks after that event, of the seventy-four who had made a commitment, some sixty-six were still living out their decision to a significant degree. From that time on, an integral part of my youth ministry has been a commitment to discipleship. In fact, all of my youth ministry (as you've seen with the funnel illustration) is discipleship and leadership-oriented. The funnel pulls young people closer to not just knowing about or experiencing Jesus, but to actually being a disciple of Jesus—one who follows Jesus' way of living, his attitudes and his perspective. As Mary, Jesus' mother, told the servants at the wedding feast (which had run out of wine), "Do whatever he tells you" (John 2:5). That's the spirit of discipleship. Our funnel should pull people toward discipleship under the influence and anointing of the Holy Spirit.

Discipleship—God's Way of Doing Things

Discipleship is a recurring theme in God's Word. The Bible tells us how discipleship happens within families, as parents bestow faith in God, obedience to God and understanding of God to their children. We see this with Abraham the patriarch, his son Isaac, Isaac's son Jacob and even with Jacob's brother Esau. Jacob (who becomes Israel), his sons (especially Joseph) and the people of God who ended up in Egypt practiced the kind of family discipleship that passes on the precepts of God and his holy lifestyle. This is evidenced by their faith that remained strong for five hundred years in a pagan country.

Joshua: A Case in Point

One early biblical example of a mature man or woman of God encouraging and training someone less mature is the relationship between Moses and young Joshua. We first meet Joshua in Exodus 17. In Exodus 17:9, Moses is preparing to battle the hostile Amalekites after struggling in the wilderness with the complaining people. Moses tells Joshua in Exodus 17:9 to "Choose some of our men and go out to fight the Amalekites. Tomorrow I will stand on top of the hill with the staff of God in my hands." So Moses interceded with God on Joshua's behalf.

The next reference to young Joshua is Exodus 24:13. By this time Joshua had become Moses' assistant and accompanied Moses to the mountain to receive the Ten Commandments. A relationship had formed between Moses, the elder statesman, and his young aide, Joshua. On that mountain Joshua witnessed Moses' intimate relationship with God as God gave the commands.

We next find young Joshua in Exodus 32. As Moses and Joshua were coming down the mount with the Ten Commandments, they heard the people singing and dancing around the golden calf. Joshua said, "There is the sound of war in the camp" (Exodus 32:17). Though Joshua had a great gift, he was mistaken. Moses gave him a better insight: "It is not the sound of victory, it is not the sound of defeat; it is the sound of singing that I hear" (Exodus 32:18). God had already spoken to Moses' heart (see Exodus 32:7-8) and told him that the people were worshiping idols. But young Joshua still had a very human perspective, devoid of the revelation one receives from spending much time with God and his Word.

Exodus 33:7-11, the next passage referring to Joshua, describes the closeness between God and Moses in the "tent of meeting." This was a special place set aside outside the camp where Moses could commune with God—a beautiful analogy of what our quiet times and devotions should be. The Bible says that the Lord would speak to Moses face to face, as a man speaks to his friend. After these sessions, Moses would return to camp, but his young aide, Joshua, did not leave the tent. So Joshua was finally beginning to enter into that intimate relationship with God that Moses had demonstrated through the years, through both the people's grumblings and their glorious victories.

One of our next glimpses into the life of Joshua is in Numbers 13 and Deuteronomy 1, where he, Caleb, a man of equal character, and ten other spies explored the promised land. You know the story. The ten reported, "It is a wonderful land, but the people are giants; we were but grasshoppers in their eyes" (author's paraphrase). They saw with human eyes only as they evaluated the huge task before them. They felt overwhelmed and defeated before they even began. But Joshua and Caleb had spent time with Moses and had seen God give victory time and time again despite insurmountable circumstances. These two told the people, "If God wants to give us the land, we can take it." After this, God swore that only Joshua and Caleb would enter the promised land while the rest of their generation would perish in the desert: "I will give him and his descendants the land he set his feet on, because he followed the Lord wholeheartedly" (Deuteronomy 1:36). This incident vividly illustrates the goal of discipleship.

In the first chapter of Joshua, the book named after this disciple, young Joshua is not young anymore. We read that, "After the death of Moses the servant of the Lord, the Lord said to Joshua son of Nun, Moses' aide: 'Moses my servant is dead. Now then, you and all these people, get ready to cross the Jordan River into the land I am about to give to them—to the Israelites. I will give you every place where you set your foot, as I promised Moses'" (Joshua 1:1-3). The discipleship process had come to its fruition, for Joshua was now a leader in charge of the people of Israel. He had been training for years, acquiring the spiritual, military and political leadership skills that God needed for that moment in history, which was crucial to God's redemptive plan. Discipleship is an essential part of what God is doing in our world.

Other Biblical Examples of Discipleship Training

But Joshua is not the only example. Throughout the Scriptures, we find the principle of discipleship at work. 1 and 2 Kings tell how Elijah trained young prophets to be spokesmen for God in their generation. The book of Daniel tells how Daniel, Shadrach, Meshach and Abednego were taught and disciplined in the pagan Babylonian schools for the strategic roles they would play in that nation's government. But more importantly, they were being discipled by God. The three also seemed to be discipled by Daniel to lead God's people. As part of God's redemptive plan, they set the stage for Jerusalem to be restored and the temple to be rebuilt so that the Messiah could one day come.

Of course, the clearest and most powerful example of discipleship in all of Scripture is Jesus. His master plan for saving the entire world was based on discipleship. Jesus did minister to the crowd, as much as he was physically able and had opportunity to do so. But we find that he spent time teaching and commissioning just seventy-two disciples (see Luke 10). He also chose twelve men whom he discipled by letting them experience God's power. Jesus spent much time teaching his disciples. As they watched, experienced, failed and succeeded, they became the team God would use to reach future generations.

In the Great Commission, (Matthew 28:19-20) Jesus commanded the seventy-two and the twelve and all who came after them to go into all the world and make disciples. We are not just to convert people, not just to lead people to an experience with God, but we are to disciple people. We are to help people bridge the gap in their lives between what they know God requires them to do and what they actually do in every facet of their lives. Also, Jesus, in his high priestly prayer in John 17:18, prays "As you sent me into the world, [to minister to the crowd, to disciple the seventy-two and especially the twelve] I have sent them into the world." Clearly, Jesus called his listeners to discipleship-oriented ministry, and that's exactly what the early Christians practiced.

Acts 2 tells how after Pentecost, during which 3,000 people were converted, the believers spent time with each other daily, having communion and fellowship and being discipled by the apostles. Paul, Silas and Barnabas, and especially Paul and young Timothy, had a discipling relationship. Paul writes to Timothy in 2 Timothy 2:2, "the things you have heard me say in the presence of many witnesses entrust to reliable men who will also be qualified to teach others." This passage refers to both discipleship and leadership training.

Discipleship Training in the Modern Church

But God's use of discipleship training didn't end with biblical times. Old Ambrose, the bishop of Milan, discipled young Augustine and produced the greatest church leader of that epoch. The genius of the Wesleyan revival was the Methodist societies, discipleship groups that met regularly and held people accountable to be committed to God, to study the Scriptures and to serve the poor.

Today the ministries of groups like The Navigators have that kind of emphasis. In the Baptist Church, discipleship continues through Barry St. Clair and much of the Baptist curriculum. The charismatic movement, though it has distorted some issues, has brought a renewed interest in discipleship. In the Wesleyan heritage, of which I'm a part, God is fostering a new interest in discipleship. I am in contact with a group of fifty or so evangelical United Methodist youth ministers who are discipleship-oriented. Discipleship is not just one component of our ministry but its very focus. We find young people are marvelously responsive to this approach.

The following is the testimony of a young man who is currently a part of a youth discipleship ministry.

Dan Searls

When I was asked to tell a bit about discipleship in my life, I thought, "This should be easy." Discipleship has been such a big part of making me the Christian I am, but I don't know where to start. I think what's helped me most is the one-on-one talk's I've had with Hule (my youth pastor) or other people on the ministry team. Getting the advice of someone who's already been through the high waters can be worth more than money at times. However, I think the discipleship I cherish the most came through the people who cared enough to hold me accountable. They shared in my victories and helped me overcome defeat. The challenge of these people helped me to take many a step closer to my Lord Jesus. Through this kind of discipleship. I wasn't given the answers. I had to work it out and decide for myself. These experiences have helped me build strong Christian character. They gave me experience and knowledge that have been priceless in my walk. I would like to encourage any of you who aren't involved in being discipled to get involved. Find a person who cares and will stretch and push you in your walk with our Lord.

Be a Disciple Yourself

Before developing a discipleship ministry in the context of a youth program, several foundations are necessary. The first is that you've got to be a disciple yourself. Merely having an academic knowledge of discipleship is not enough to launch a discipleship ministry among young people. The old adage that you can't lead anyone further than you've been yourself is the absolute truth when it comes to ministering to young people.

Youth ministers who cling to an old experience in college or remember past times of learning and discipleship will find this is not sufficient to sustain a cutting edge, a discipleship-oriented youth program. One must be involved with discipleship in an ongoing way, not only in one's personal time with God but also in interrelationships with other parts of the body of Christ—church staff, family, the community and other pastors or youth workers. We need the accountability, challenge and tutorage of discipleship in our own lives. From this current experience and from biblical convictions, we can then bring our young people a personal, relational and discipleship ministry.

Catch the Vision of Discipleship

Another essential foundation for an effective discipleship program is to catch the vision of discipleship in the context of youth ministry. At the grow level (described in the last chapter) we try to teach youth the great principles of who God is and what God wants of us in our daily lives. While learning these concepts and growing and relating to God, many youth feel a new, passionate desire to know God and to please God. They also become aware that their lives don't measure up to God's high calling.

Bridging the Gap

This tension in our lives is defined by many writers as the dialectic tension between the ideal self and the real self. We all face this conflict, whether or not we are Christians. But this tension is especially acute in the life of a young Christian.

I used to feel rather guilty about helping create such tension. God's standards seem so unachievable for young people. I was sometimes accused of creating a "guilt trip" for youth.

At first, I had no response to this criticism other than to say I felt I was taking the biblical approach to life. But I finally received assurance about this aspect of ministry from an unlikely source Tony Campolo pointed out—an atheist, a radical sociologist named Marcuse. Some of you may be unfamiliar with Marcuse, but you have heard of one of his disciples, Angela Davis, who was part of the black radical movement during the 1960s. Many blacks in those days looked to her for her radical ideas, for her deep desire for revolution in our country and for a new start for blacks and other minorities. Marcuse was in a sense her master, the one who discipled her.

Marcuse accused the American government of relaxing the standards for our culture during that period. He noted that our mores and cultural values were so weak that almost anything was acceptable. The hallmark of those days was: "If it feels good, do it. If it turns you on, do it. Even if you disagree with what someone else does, keep your mouth shut and let them do their thing, and you do your thing." Marcuse said the government had done this on purpose, because when the dialectic tension between the ideal self and the real self is diminished, so is the will to revolt and the impetus for social movement and individual development. This creates an apathetic vacuum—a narcissistic boredom resulting in a lack of motivation.[1]

When I read this, I suddenly felt justified about calling young people to deny themselves daily, to pick up their crosses and to follow Jesus. I felt vindicated for alerting them to the high call of Christ that Paul wrote about and to the whole concept of Christian perfection. Because in the very struggle between the ideal self and the real self is born the spiritual and emotional energy and movement needed for effective change and growth. Bridging the gap between what our young people know they ought to be and what they should do, and between what they are and what they are doing, is the goal of discipleship ministry.

As we help young people bridge that gap, we also create in them a new confidence. This is not faith in their own willpower or I-can-do spirit. Rather, it's a new faith and trust in the grace of God and his ability to change and transform their hearts.

Other Goals of Discipleship

Another goal of discipleship ministry is to promote accountability. We should create in our young people not only the willingness but also the desire to be accountable for their actions. We must teach them not to perpetuate that spirit of hell which started in the Garden of Eden, that causes us to blame each other or rationalize away our misdeeds or lack of motivation. We are accountable to God and to others to be what we ought to be, to do what we say we will do. To put it another way, one of our goals is to build accountability in the community of faith.

Another goal is to create an attitude and lifestyle of commitment and service. Our young people must understand that Christianity is not simply an experience. The Christian faith is not a product of Western culture but an attitude of service and a lifestyle of following the Lord Jesus Christ.

We also want to help our young people adopt a world-changing, life-changing perspective through the process of discipleship. We must help our young people extend their walks and relationships with God to their schools, on dates, at home, on the athletic court or field, or in any academic, social and economic arena. The cutting edge of their relationship with God is not cloistered in the sanctuary, cloaked by the cultural mores of the day. Rather, faith is to be lived day in and day out. It's a life-changing, world-changing walk with the world changer, the Lord Jesus Christ.

Learn the Methods and Approaches to Discipleship

Another essential foundation we need before starting discipleship ministry is to understand some basic methods and approaches. The tenor of discipleship is relational. Relationship is the bridge over which discipleship flows, both as the disciple-maker shares wisdom and life experiences with the person being discipled and as the disciple questions and observes the disciple-maker. Even programmatic discipleship must include that relational quality or it will be ineffective at fostering discipleship.

There are basically two approaches to discipleship. One is to chose people who are natural leaders, young people who are recognized as leaders on the campus, the football field and the church. Campus Crusade for Christ and Youth For Christ, in my opinion seem to favor this approach. They find and disciple youth leaders who can then disciple others. I think there is scriptural validity in this approach; it follows Paul's instructions to Timothy in 2 Timothy 2:2—to find "reliable men."

The other approach to discipleship is that of "whosoever will." This means that we disciple whoever is willing to be a disciple regardless of his or her leadership potential. Certainly, that was Jesus' method of doing discipleship. It's been the church's method through the years, and I find that my ministry most often takes this approach.

One-on-One Discipleship

There are four basic methods of discipleship training. First is the one-on-one relationship method. In this discipleship style we may, for example, use some study materials and meet with a person at breakfast to build a one-on-one relationship. This way of discipling fits that person's need at the moment.

I find this is the most powerful method available. It is certainly the method of the family—Mom and Dad interacting with the young person. This type of relationship can exist between a youth minister or pastor and a young person. It even works as seniors and juniors meet with sixth through eighth graders one-on-one, praying and holding each other accountable.

An approach entitled *The Onward Bound Program* adapts the one-on-one method and focuses on the particular needs of the young person being discipled. I learned about this program from the previous youth minister at Wilmore United Methodist Church, Duffy Robbins. We've reprinted on page 119 a copy of the Onward Bound Growth Contract. This contract allows the adult counselor or parent—or whoever is using the program—to help the young person select character goals to work on. These can be positive or negative goals. For example, the person might want to become a better witness at home, stop fighting with parents or quit cursing or lusting. Then the disciple-maker, working perhaps with the minister or parents prescribes weekly exercises to help the young disciple achieve his or her goals.

Remember, we're trying to help young people bridge the gap between what they know and what they do. The Onward Bound prescriptions in the sample contract include Scripture memorization and study and reading from a book that relates to the area of concern in the young person's life. Youth are also assigned projects each week that are designed to help bridge the gap between the ideal person God calls them to be and the real person they are today. This is an excellent approach to one-on-one discipleship.

Discipleship, Small Group Style

Another helpful approach is small group discipleship. In this method a group of three to six people meet because of a common desire for discipleship. Each person might have his or her own prescribed goals and character motivations to work on, for which groups members hold each other accountable. The group could be built around a certain study guide or overall goal such as becoming better witnesses, understanding the will of God or having quiet times of personal devotion with God.

Small group ministry is a very valuable part of our discipleship program. For example, our "Marines Program" has been very effective with young men who have a great desire to be macho and to be pushed beyond their limits. This discipleship program uses that desire for the kingdom of God by giving them a Marine-type regimen which holds them accountable for daily disciplines such as prayer, Bible study, Scripture memory, academic work, family time and social time. We also challenge them to strengthen their bodies though rigorous physical exercise. This helps them enhance their self-image and ability to protect themselves (as well as lessen their need to prove themselves in negative aggression) by giving them training in various sports or martial arts. We increase their ability to reach out to others by giving them challenging projects in which they serve others. As you can see, small group discipleship is an exciting concept.

Onward Bound Growth Contract

"I do not claim that I have already become perfect. I press on for the prize of the upward call of God in Christ Jesus. Of course, my brothers, I really do not think that I have made it; the one thing I do, however, is to forget what lies behind me and do my best to reach what lies ahead . . ." (Philippians 3:12-14).

Date _January 1_

Please complete this growth contract carefully, prayerfully and completely. This is a covenant, a contract, a PROMISE, that to the best of your ability, with God's help, you will complete the contract below. This contract is based on areas of growth that you have pin-pointed for special concentration. Be willing to push yourself. Your Growth Partner is taking valuable time to meet with you. Make those meetings count. Try to meet with him/her a minimum of three times, four times if possible.

I, _Jane_ in an effort to "press on for the prize of the upward call of God in Christ Jesus," do solemnly commit myself, with God's help, to grow in the following areas of my life. I understand that I will be held accountable for these goals and that my contract to grow in these areas is not to be taken lightly.

Remember: Be Specific! Character Goal One: _self-control in thoughts_
Character Goal Two: _genuine concern for pagan friends_

It is my responsibility to meet with my growth partner, _Ann_ I will be responsible for setting up meetings on the following days/times;

#1 _January 15 — 3 p.m._
#2 _January 29 — 4 p.m._
#3 _February 12 — 4 p.m._
#4 _February 27 — 3 p.m._

This contract is to be finished by _3-1_ (Date).

In order to make progress toward these goals I have stated, I will work in the following growth areas with the assignments listed below.

Character Projects:

Week 1-2 _1) memorize Rom. 12:1-2 2) record negative thoughts_
Week 2-3 _1) read Gal. 5:16-23 2) read ch. 1-3 of "Renewed Mind"_
Week 4-5 _1) pray 15 min. for pagan friends 2) rewrite "Prodigal Son"_
Week 6-7 _record "unrenewed thinking" for 3 days; note improvement_
Service Project (LT II) _Do overt good for each pagan friend._

I will do my best "to reach what lies ahead . . ."

Signature _Jane Smith_

Prayer and Share Discipleship

Another especially effective form of discipleship training is the prayer and share program, or covenant group, approach. Again, I learned these names and concepts from Duffy Robbins, though I had used some of them at Tyler Street under different names and with a slightly different organization.

The covenant group is a fairly large group of people who meet together. Each person in the group is responsible for keeping a journal and following an Onward Bound contract. Participants are personally accountable for their own quiet times and journal keeping. They also work on character and life-related projects and are required to attend every week. Our covenant group meets at 6:15 in the morning, which makes it difficult and discipleship-oriented. The group members read from their journals and share their prayer concerns, successes and failures. Because group members support each other, they experience the *koinonia* (fellowship) that gives them a new measure of strength and ability to be God's disciples.

Discipleship Specials

In addition to the three methods of discipleship training we've just discussed, discipleship specials are also very effective. A discipleship special may take the form of a spiritual life retreat in which the focus is not calling people to Christ or to grow, but to deepen one's commitment to God and further one's walk with Christ.

In my ministry, stress camps are one of the most successful discipleship specials. Stress camps create a real life opportunity for young people to apply the Word of God. They use the scriptural precepts they've learned as they live under the stress of conflict with others and in sometimes excruciating circumstances in the wilderness. This is an exciting concept in discipleship training that you can pursue with proper training.

Mission trips present another opportunity for hands-on, experiential discipleship learning. We take two a year. One mission trip takes place in our own state—a Kentucky event. The other is cross-cultural. By actively reaching out to others, our young people have a chance to live out Jesus' command to love one another. By doing so, they let people know that they are his disciples. On mission trips, youth grow through serving people of other cultures. They learn in a thousand different ways how to live the faith that they profess.

Beware the Dangers of Discipleship Training

Another foundation that should be laid before beginning a discipleship ministry is to understand the common pitfalls of a discipleship level program in youth ministry.

The Exclusive Club Syndrome. One common problem is division in the group. Although you certainly don't intend to do so, you sometimes create groups of spiritual haves and have-nots—young people who are in discipleship training and those who choose not to be. Discipleship can become a kind of exclusive holy club that fosters feelings of disunity. We must be sensitive to the division that discipleship ministry naturally brings because it differentiates between people in a more dramatic way than the come or grow levels do. It is often difficult to discern exactly who is in those levels. Many young people who come on Sunday night will also be there on Wednesday night, attending both come and grow level events. But the discipleship commitment distinguishes certain young people from the others in the group.

The best solution to this problem is to keep the discipleship program low-key. Challenge the young people to only be identified as disciples by their service. They should not be vocal about being in the discipleship program but should let their lives do the talking. This attitude reflects the spirit of discipleship anyway.

Pharisaism. Another problem that can arise is Pharisaism. It emerges when a program or the very act of discipleship becomes an end in itself. When the group prides itself on keeping rules, and equates that with being a disciple, it is substituting form for substance. Pharisaism allows a young person to salve his or her conscience about not being accountable to God or serving others because he or she is in a discipleship program.

Pharisaism can be arrested by maintaining the personal touch. Hold disciples accountable not just to memorize Bible verses and have six quiet times a week, but to be sensitive to parents, be a witness at school and overcome habits that destroy their relationship with God and other people.

Guruism. Another problem that often happens in discipleship training is the emergence of what I call "guruism."

I'll never forget the first time I met Ben Lester. Ben was a Youth For Christ director in Southern California for about fifteen years, where he also worked with the Fellowship of Christian Athletes. Ben was interesting because of his experience and personality. He told me how over the years he'd learned a few things, and one of them was that we can have a life-long impact on only a few individuals. Our ministries will have some benefit for those at the come and grow levels. But only on the discipleship/leadership levels, where we work with fewer people, are we able to affect young people for a lifetime.

He also mentioned that he didn't want his ministry to produce young people who were spiritual gurus. At first I was taken aback because I thought he meant that he didn't want people to be totally committed to God or totally consumed by their relationship with God. But the more I thought about what he said, the more I realized that this is a danger we face in our discipling programs.

We need to be careful not to produce one-sided young people who spiritualize absolutely every dimension of life. For such people, anything that is not spiritual is sinful. They see involvement in sports, for example, as somehow less than the best. To them, enjoying relationships with other people that don't revolve around a spiritual topic is somehow entering a gray area. Enjoying God's gifts, such as nature, food or hard work, is somehow less valuable than the spiritual best of prayer and teaching others about God. These gurus correctly make Jesus the center of life, but they develop an imbalance so that all of life not strictly perceived as being in the spiritual realm is somehow less than the best.

Certainly, we don't need these kinds of gurus in our youth group. We want young people who have the sense of wholeness and balance that God brings to our lives and has so freely given us through his creation.

Spiritual Parasitism. A final danger is "spiritual parasitism." This occurs when we make our youth so dependent on being in some sort of discipleship program that they lose their ability to initiate and maintain their relationships with God. Young people who are spiritual parasites have no motivation to rely on God for victory over life- and witness-destroying habits and sin. So we must be sure our discipleship process helps young people stand alone as well as enjoy the benefits of accountability to and support from others.

Where Do We Begin?

After we lay the foundations—we understand that we have to be disciples ourselves, we catch the goals and visions of discipleship ministry, we learn some helpful approaches, and we recognize some common dangers—we're ready to begin our discipleship program. Whether you are a pastor in a small church or a youth minister in charge of hundreds of young people, how do you develop discipleship programs where you are?

Let's examine some general principles to help you get started. Of course, it's up to each individual minister to formulate, with God's guidance, the discipleship program that will bring the results the Scriptures and the Holy Spirit desire in people's lives.

Start in Your Own Corner

The first thing to do when developing a discipleship level program is to start where you are. Begin with the relationships that you already have, in your unique environment and culture.

We can observe three Ds to help us start where we are. First, we must **discern** our situation—our givens, our gifts and our goofs. Each situation has its own unique characteristics.

Maybe your theological and philosophical perspectives lend themselves beautifully to discipleship, so that it's a natural outgrowth of your ministry. Or perhaps the tradition in which you serve considers discipleship a new, suspicious and risky idea. Maybe your church has had some bad experiences in discipleship ministry, and people are not very open to it. In this case, progress will be slow and meticulous. But whatever your milieu, you need to discern your givens.

You also need to discern the things that will undermine discipleship. You're going to have to discern the negative feelings that may arise as you launch your discipleship program.

Perhaps even more difficult, you need to try to discern your own gifts and the gifts of those to whom you want to offer this discipleship program. Which of God's gifts are available to you as abilities, materials and tools for use in your discipleship training?

The second "D" is to **discover** your youth. You can best do this by getting to know as many of your young people as possible. Each youth minister, in any given situation, ought to methodically maintain a list or card file with youths' names. Each week, hold yourself accountable to meet one-on-one with different youth so that you meet personally with every youth in your youth group in one or two years' time. For example, I hold myself accountable to meet with six young people each week. This pulls me into their lives so that I can better discover their openness to discipleship and their level of involvement with Christ, the youth group, their parents and life itself. You must discover your youths' openness and maturity levels so that you can better plan your discipleship ministry.

The last "D" is to **develop** your program at a pace and in a style that fits your church's chemistry. All churches and youth ministries have their assets and liabilities. Sometimes a discipleship program will almost develop itself, while at other churches and at other times all one can do is plant seeds for a future discipleship ministry.

With Whom Do We Begin?

After you discern your situation, discover where your youth are and develop your program to fit your church, you are ready to choose young people who are ready for discipleship. The natural place to start is with the young people in your group who fit some general characteristics. Using the word "disciple" as an acrostic, I offer some guidelines to help determine the type of young person who hungers for discipleship ministry.

D–*Direct* prayer toward your youth. This is always the place to start any ministry—in prayer. As you pray through the names on your list or file cards, or whatever method you use, saturate your discipleship program in prayer. Open yourself to God, to the Scriptures and to what you know of the lives of the young people. Make a list of those with whom you already have a relationship, who you feel are ready to be introduced to the particular discipleship program and approach that you plan to use.

I–Find young people who are *interested.* Discipleship will not work with disinterested youth. Young people should not be arm-twisted into joining a discipleship program. It ought to be a relational ministry or program for those who are interested and should never be compulsory.

S—Look for young people who are *submissive.* "Submissive" is not one of my favorite words, but it does describe the kind of attitude a disciple needs. A young person should be willing to submit himself or herself to God and to following the call and the character of Christ. This submission might better be described by saying such a young person is not rebellious. Rebellion is water poured on the fire of discipleship, while submission is gasoline added to that flame.

C—A young disciple should be *committed.* A young person must be willing and committed to obey Christ and to grow. A disciple is not only ready to change direction and face God but is also willing to step out and walk with Christ.

I—Select a young person who is an *initiator.* Such an individual will take initiative and exert effort to move toward Christ through the discipleship process.

P—Choose disciples who are *persevering.* A young person who's tough and is mentally and emotionally mature enough to persevere, pay a price and remember "no pain, no gain" will be a good disciple.

L—Look for a *learner,* someone who is teachable. Such a youth is not only willing and committed but also has a learner's heart. He or she is humble and doesn't claim to know it all or to have achieved everything. Disciples need to be poor in spirit in their attitudes, so that they feel the need to learn and develop.

E—Choose people who will make an *effort*. Good disciples will go the second mile, even when they fail or are frustrated. When things don't seem to be working, these people still give an honest effort.

What Do We Do?

After you have an idea of what type of youth you're looking for, you must decide what to do. How do you get your discipleship level ministry off the ground?

I suggest you start with the young person in your church's milieu who fits the description of a disciple and with whom you already have a relationship. Evaluate your youth group and try to discern how many of those young people are ready for discipleship. Then calculate how many disciple-makers you have in your church with whom to do discipleship training. I strongly encourage you to do this in a one-on-one, informal manner. For example, let's say that "Judy" is coming to Bible study and seems hungry for spiritual things. She comes to you for prayer about struggles she's having being a Christian at home and tells you about the victory she's having in sharing Jesus with her friends. You see the qualities of a disciple in her, and you want to encourage and support her. You might say to her, "Judy, my wife and I would like to have you over for dinner" (or breakfast or a coke or a pizza), or you could invite her to talk to you after youth meeting.

When you get together, tell Judy that you and your wife (if you are a man) would like to start meeting with her. (I strongly encourage men to meet with men and women to meet with women. If you plan to disciple an opposite-sex young person, include your spouse or other opposite-sex friend in your meetings.) Ask Judy if she'd be willing to meet for seven weeks and use a Navigators book, the Churches Alive curriculum or some other prescribed, planned study. Tell Judy, "We're going to go through this material together, and I want to give you some projects that will help you be the woman of God you want to be. This will help you be victorious in some of your struggles. Are you willing to meet with me (or us) to work on that?"

I wouldn't call this discipleship or label it as a program. Simply begin to meet with young people who are ready. Most of them will be glad to do so. You might want to encourage other people on your ministry team or in your church to do the same thing with young people in your group. Each adult ought to be able to handle two to three one-on-one discipleship relationships per seven-week term.

If you have more interested young people than you have adults who can meet one-on-one with them, you might want to announce a discipleship group event at your grow level Bible study. Always announce your next level of ministry at the one above it. It's probably not a good idea to announce your discipleship group at a come level event because some people might want to attend for social reasons or will misunderstand what it's all about and this can create an uncomfortable situation. But at your Bible study, announce something like this: "On Tuesday morning at 6:00 we're going to get together to pray for one another, encourage one another, challenge one another and give each other projects to help us grow and develop our Christian walk. If you'd like to join that kind of group, I encourage you to come."

Say six to eight young people show up. Assign them disciplines that they'll be accountable for and committed to. This is the beginning of your discipleship group or program.

There are a million other ways to start a discipleship ministry. You can gather small groups of young people for a session about how to know God's will and apply it to one's life or how to overcome sin. Or you can plan a group session as a elective course during Sunday school class or as an alternative to Bible study if you've got enough people to do so. But I find that scheduling discipleship training at times when other meetings are not in progress is much more low key and causes less division.

What Materials Do We Use?

After you have set up a meeting time, you must decide

what kind of curriculum or study materials to use in your discipleship training.

Certainly, the Bible is your best resource, your prime tool in discipleship. We want our young people to be able to receive instruction, challenge, perspective and attitudinal help from God's Word. Discipleship training certainly involves memorizing Scripture, discussing the Bible and exploring Scripture case studies.

We want to involve the Scriptures at every turn, but many Scripture study aids can also help us with our small groups and our one-on-one discipleship. Several groups offer excellent discipleship materials. Foremost in my mind is the Navigator's *Design for Discipleship Books 1-10* series. Another parachurch organization offering excellent material for discipleship is Campus Crusade for Christ, which publishes several series on Christian maturity and discipleship. Barry St. Clair and his *Student Venture* material is another tremendous source of good discipleship material. For the covenant group approach, the Onward Bound program described in *Building a Discipleship Ministry in the Local Church* by Duffy Robbins is an excellent resource, (it is a Scripture Press Power Pack booklet). Dawson McAllister's *Discipleship Guide I, II, and III* and *Walk to the Cross* are also outstanding discipleship materials.

Most evangelical curriculum series can be adapted for discipleship training. Many InterVarsity and Navigators books on friendship, evangelism and other topics are excellent sources. Gordon MacDonald's *Ordering Your Private World* can even be fashioned to a discipleship event. *The Pursuit of Holiness* and *The Pursuit of Godliness* by Jerry Bridges (and their study guides) are other excellent sources for discipleship groups.

How Long Does It Last?

How long should a discipleship group meet? Seven C's can help us grasp the rhythm and the process of discipleship ministry.

■ **Contact** the person or group you've selected, either personally or announcing it at your grow level Bible study.

■ **Connect** with those people. Learn their needs. Meet

with them. At your first get-together find out where they're at. Then build connections.

■ **Call** them. Challenge them to join you or others for seven weeks. You not only call them, but you also ask them to commit and consecrate themselves for a specific time period. I find seven weeks is a good length of time to meet. That's long enough to develop real character and a sense of accomplishment but not so long that it seems like it's lasting forever. Seven weeks of discipleship training allows enough time for young people to see how much they've learned and how far they have come in their walk with God. Our ministry generally offers seven-week discipleship cycles about three to five times a year. These use different methods and approaches and cover the various seasons.

■ **Challenge** your disciples to radical Christianity— there really is no other kind. Challenge them to accept the high call of Christ. Focus on what Jesus calls us to be and do.

■ **Condition** youth to carry on what they're learning after your seven-week period of discipleship training ends. They should make discipleship a part of their lifestyles so that it's not just an empty ritual like the Pharisees' behavior. Challenge them to make discipleship the substance of their lives.

■ **Commission** them to commit themselves to discipleship that they initiate themselves. They should meet with their friends and disciple and encourage each other, holding each other accountable.

■ After you have lead discipleship series for a time — seven weeks on, seven weeks off, special events, and retreats—you see God change young people. Kids who know what they ought to do but are frustrated and failing became mature, world-changing, self-motivating men and women of God. It's very important that about every year you **commend** them. Write them a note, encourage them, tell them how proud you are of them and how much you rejoice in the ministry that God has given them.

Have We Hit the Target?

How do you evaluate your discipleship ministry? It is a

subjective endeavor, to be sure. How can we evaluate spiritual growth?

Although it's difficult, we *can* ask certain objective questions about our discipleship program: (1) Do young people attend, are they interested, does it relate to their lives? (2) Have there been any detectable or recordable changes in their lives? (3) Has it achieved the desired result—to create disciples of Christ?

We also must remember, as we study the how-to's of discipleship ministry, that no single method or approach is always best. In fact, as we mature in our discipling we begin to use several methods in concert. At times, we may be using four to six discipleship groups and relationships at once. Such a symphony of discipleship training approaches can meet the needs of both the group and individuals.

7 Leadership

Training Youth to Be the Disciplers of Others

By Hule Goddard

Marx said that leadership is the struggle for the hearts and minds of youth. All over the world today the struggle for their hearts, minds, attention, money, allegiance and time continues. People, including young people, are going to be led by someone or something, whether communism, the media, Hari Krishna, Mohammed, Buddha or Jesus Christ, the Son of the Living God.

We in youth ministry must not fail to develop leadership in our young people. We cannot simply ask young people to commit their lives to Christ, to study God's way, to become disciples of the Lord Jesus and stop there. We must fulfill the entire Great Commission. We must make clear that the greatest leader in the kingdom of God is the greatest servant. We have a command from God that demands that we be involved in leadership development ministry.

Beware the One-Sided Faith

While serving in Dallas, I first began to understand the need for leadership training as part of youth ministry. There I found a group of young people who had received the best that evangelical Christianity had to offer. They had speakers and concerts and mission trips and choir tours.

Time after time, they enjoyed wonderful revival experiences and basked in God's presence.

After I had been there a few months, we experienced one of those times when God's blessing was poured out on the group. But I found that afterwards the young people's attitude was, "Wow, God, that was good. What's next?"

As I worked with this group, I began to realize that these young people were bored. They lacked passion, and the antagonism and self-centeredness in many of their lives didn't reflect the character of the Lord Jesus. I began to see that this was because they were one-sided Christians. They were always receiving, always focusing on their relationship with God and his blessing them, healing them and being their counselor. This was all good, but I struggled to think of ways to involve those young people in serving others, the second half of God's command to "love me, and love others."

I began by involving the youth in small ways, such as teaching a junior high Bible study. Suddenly, the youth became interested in the junior high kids and developed a new interest in Bible study that went beyond their own personal edification. The gained a new feeling of ownership in the youth group and felt a new excitement.

I took a group of these young people to present a seminar on sex and dating to some five hundred youth. Our young people presented skits and gave testimonies about how they had begun a new way of life and what it meant to be a Christian. At last, these youth were giving as well as taking. As young people all over the auditorium made spontaneous commitments at the end of that seminar, I was thrilled about what the Spirit of God was doing among them. But I was even more thrilled that as every commitment was made, the young people who had lead the seminar sat higher and higher in their seats. A glow came over them. These young people no longer had to be urged and pushed into serving others, for they had experienced the joy and wonder of God's using us earthen vessels.

Since then I have found that young people are anxious to be involved in what God is doing in the world. I've seen young people share the gospel on mission trips and lead many people to salvation. I've seen young people feed the hungry in other countries and rebuild houses in downtown Lexington for needy people. Young people have a great capacity for service if they are issued the call, given the opportunity to serve and receive some basic training.

Leadership level ministry is not just a luxury for a few marine-like youth groups; it is God's call for his Church. I am convinced that my experience with self-centered, bored kids is not unique. Tony Campolo notes that Western society no longer allows young people to fill heroic roles or meet vocational challenges that are worthy of their humanity or that make the Christian worthy of being a child of God.[1]

In our culture young people indulge themselves in pleasure and in egocentric, money-making careers only to find themselves bored and without passion. Søren Kierkegaard laments, "Let others complain that the age is wicked; my complaint is that it's wretched for it lacks passion."[2] One of the hallmarks of Western culture in the 1970s and 1980s is the lack of vision for a better world. Somehow, this vision died with the great liberal dream of the 1960s and has been replaced by a lack of hope about the future.

God Still Calls Heroes

I believe one of the most important calls of God upon the church today, particularly upon youth ministry, is for us to challenge young people to the kind of leadership that causes one to lay down his or her life for God's purposes, to enter a vocation to serve others and to make the world a place where children can grow up healthy rather than sick and hungry. The church today must train young people to be like Jesus, whose life and teachings taught us that the person who is the greatest is also the greatest servant.

Evidently, Leighton Ford, the chairman of the Lusanne Committee for World Evangelism, agrees. He feels that one of the paramount challenges facing the church is mobilizing gifted young people from our own ranks to be in the forefront of God's initiative as this century closes.[3]

Raising up leaders and calling the church to raise up leaders is something God has always done. In the Scriptures we find that whenever God wants to do a significant work in our world, a baby is born. That leader is then trained and commissioned to accomplish God's task. Noah, Abraham, Joseph, Moses, Joshua, Samson, Samuel, David, Ezra, Nehemiah, Isaiah, Nathan, Haggai and the minor prophets are vivid examples of this. When God wanted to rescue his people and make his ways and himself clear, he became a baby and a man in the person of Jesus Christ, whose life models for us what leadership is all about.

Jesus' teaching on leadership is very clear. In the world, he points out, leadership means lording it over others, but in the kingdom of God leadership is demonstrated through faithful service and genuine love for God and people (Matthew 20:25-28). Although Jesus sent out as many as seventy-two followers at one time, (see Luke 10) he had twelve close disciples and three specific disciples (Peter, James and John) whom he trained to lead the new church. Sure enough, in the book of Acts we find that Peter, James, John and, as one born beyond the proper time, Paul successfully guided the early church in the ways of God.

This emphasis on leadership continued in the early church as Ambrose trained young Augustine. At every point of genuine need in the church, God has raised up a leader such as St. Francis of Assisi, Martin Luther, John Wesley or Francis Asbury. God still raises up young men and women today. Tom Holman is a member of our youth group, and God's hand is upon him, preparing him, I am convinced, for leadership. But let Tom explain what leadership training means to him.

Tom Holman

Being in a leadership program in my youth group was an excellent experience for me. It helped me develop in so many areas that are essential to being a leader.

I learned how to be more disciplined through being accountable for different things that I needed to work on in my life. Also, I'd learned responsibility and how to handle situations as they came up. Through weekly meetings and special trips I was taught how to deal with others and how to disciple them in their growth.

But most importantly I learned how to effectivly share the love of Jesus with others on a personal level (just sharing one on one) or in front of a whole group of people.

I was able to lead a small group in which a friend my age and I met with several younger guys once or twice a week to grow and have fellowship. We led the group in many activities such as fishing or camping in the woods. This was a lot of fun but we also grew together and were able to share our struggles and victories as we lived out our lives for Jesus in the way he wants us to.

The things that I learned going through that leadership program have helped me time and again as I walk with the Lord. I know that it will help me in the future because I will be able to fall back on all that I learned, and the qualities that it put into me will help me in the long run. I am so glad that it was available to me.

Scripture, church history and common experience tell us that the work of the Holy Spirit is to raise up leaders to inspire and guide people in God's ways for a particular generation. Therefore, our youth programming must include opportunities for young people to develop as Christian leaders in their vocations, homes, nation and families.

Developing Leadership Qualities in Youth

To build an effective leadership training level program, we need to understand some basic concepts. We need to grasp the goals and the nature of Christian leadership. We need to understand the three components of leadership. We need to recognize the advantages and limitations of teenage leadership development. And we need to be alert to the common dangers of leadership training within the context of youth ministry.

What Exactly is Leadership Training?

First, we need to understand the visions, goals and nature of Christian leadership. Leadership training helps a person develop his or her God-given personality and gifts, as well as the ability, confidence, character and skill to use these gifts to serve God and others. Jesus clearly defines Christian leadership as servanthood. In Matthew 23:8-12 Jesus says we are to let no one call us Rabbi, father or teacher because, "you have one Teacher, the Christ. The greatest among you will be your servant."

Like Jesus, the apostle Paul explains that servanthood is a hallmark of leadership. In Philippians 2:5-7 Paul encourages the Christians in Philippi and today: "Your attitude should be the same as that of Christ Jesus: Who, being in very nature God, did not consider equality with God something to be grasped, but made himself nothing, taking the very nature of a servant. . . ."

Thus, the goals of Christian leadership are (1) to call every young person to a lifestyle of servanthood to God and to others, (2) to help every youth build a Christlike character as the basis for genuine love and service, (3) to help each youth discover his or her unique temperament, grace and abilities so that he or she can be used effectively in service to God and others, (4) to equip every youth with the basic skills needed to serve God and others, (5) to provide young people with a progressing experience in Christian leadership and (6) to challenge young people to choose vocations that best serve God and other people.

What Are the Three Components of Leadership?

After we understand the basic goals of Christian leadership, we need to study its components, which I've identified as character, skill and experience. Effective Christian leadership is impossible without the combination of these three attributes.

Building Character. Christlike character is best defined as a lifestyle that springs from attitudes and convictions that result from a personal, daily relationship with Jesus Christ.

People are generally led by fear or respect. Government, for example, exists either because of exterior factors such as pain or pleasure, or interior forces such as love, respect and conviction. Christian leaders must possess the character of Christ in order to live consistent lives of love and service. These exemplary lives earn the respect of others, and this respect is the basis of Christian leadership. Thus, one of the cornerstones of leadership is character.

Developing Skill. Another component of leadership is skill. Leadership skill basically involves the abilities necessary to be an effective Christian leader. Without certain basic human relations skills in communication, teaching, disciplining, counseling, problem solving and conflict management, doing ministry is like cutting with a dull knife. It's possible, but it can be inefficient and frustrating.

Gaining Experience. An effective Christian leader also needs experience. The church today offers us much teaching about Christian character. We can even gain some skill, for example, in sharing our testimony or reaching others with the spoken Word of Christ. But the church gives us very little opportunity to experience Christian leadership. We're like an army of trained soldiers who have not been tried in battle. We don't know what's going to happen when the heat of battle comes. We know mistakes will be made, and we pray that they are not mistakes that jeopardize the soldier's future or the outcome of the war.

Young people need experience to refine and strengthen their Christlike character, and only practical experience will sharpen the skill they've learned. Experience gives young people the confidence and the competence they need to bring God glory by bringing others to a personal relationship with God and ministering to their needs.

What Are the Blessings and Pitfalls of Leadership Training for Teens?

Most great Olympic stars start training at a very early age. Ice skaters and gymnasts often begin training at age six or younger so that when they come of age they can win the gold medal. How much more important it is to start the training process at an early age for an even greater medal! But to build an effective leadership training level ministry we must understand the advantages and the limitations of teenage leadership training.

Somehow, we've gotten the idea that youth is not an age for serious service to God. Instead, we invent a kind of holding area for young people where they can wait until they're adults and can then be effectively trained for service. But I think some advantages exist in doing leadership training in youth ministry.

Advantages of Leadership Training for Youth

Let's look first at the advantages. Teenagers are in a formative, idealistic stage in their lives. I think they are in the second best stage of life for training with age zero through two being the most strategic time. But in reference to leadership, I believe that youth are in the prime of their lives for training.

Young people are forming ideas about themselves, their beliefs and their goals. What better time for us to train them to make their lives count for Jesus, to become servants who will minister to the world's needs? Also, during the teenage years, youth are very idealistic. They will give themselves energetically to causes they believe are right. What better time is there to call young people to Christian leadership?

We find that teenagers are already in a training stage—another plus. In every area of life, they are learning discipline. They are training at school in academics and at home in other areas—spiritual, relational, romantic, etc. They are being trained in the various clubs and athletic groups they join at school. For the most part, youth are undergoing a molding process. What better time for us as the church to train our young people to be Christian leaders?

Another advantage is that young people are able. They are emotionally, physically, mentally and spiritually capable of great accomplishments in the service of God. They may be better able now than at any other time in their lives to do God's work, though they do usually need more maturity and balance. They certainly can be effective Christian leaders.

Limitations of Leadership Training for Youth

We need to understand some limitations of a leadership training program in our youth group. One of these is that young people are in a stage of transition. As their hormones, emotions and self-concepts are in the process of maturing, they can be unstable. They tend toward romantic and relational disasters and binges in various areas of sin and misunderstanding.

Youth often have difficulty with their sense of balance and perspective. They may have great zeal but little knowledge and experience. Their passion, like a wild prairie fire, may even burn them as it moves them to serve God and mankind.

Young people are also under their parents' and teachers' authority. We as youth ministers only have access to this authority as it is bestowed upon us by parents. We can only work effectively to the degree that Mom and Dad will allow us to do so. At times, this is a great limitation. For example, some parents have visions and convictions that differ from those of the body of Christ and the biblical point of view.

What Are the Dangers of Leadership Level Ministry?

We need to understand the common dangers inherent in youth ministry leadership training. These are similar to the dangers involved in discipleship training.

Leadership training in youth ministry sometimes creates a kind of Christian bourgeoisie, or Christian "haves" and "have nots." When this happens, the leaders have the status, and they appear to be doing all the work. Other kids, who perhaps haven't come to Christ in a significant way, or whose commitment is still developing, or who are just trying to mature and become stable in their walk with Christ, may feel put down or left out. Leadership training can create divisions in a youth group.

Another danger of leadership training is that as we involve young people in ministry to others, we place them at risk of failure. Young people will sometimes become discouraged and afraid to try again because of their frustration at not being as effective as they had hoped they would be.

Another problem in leadership training of young people is over-commitment. Never before in the history of my ministry have I seen so much stress placed on teenagers. In Sunday school and Bible study, I find myself teaching subjects like stress and time management and how to simplify one's life. That certainly was not the case when I started youth ministry fifteen years ago. In our day of heightened educational demands, increased athletic expectations and expanding job requirements, young people are running into problems similar to those facing business executives, burned-out housewives and ministers in their thirties and forties.

Building character takes time. Learning skills takes time, as does hands-on involvement in the lives of other people. It cannot be regulated with a clock. We must not overload our young people with so many things to do that we give them a feeling of hopelessness.

Another common danger is that as young people assume leadership in the youth group, community and school, it is easy for them to adopt the attitude of the world. As Jesus said, "the rulers of the Gentiles lord it over them" (Matthew 20:25). Leadership can become an ego matter when the focus is on the status of being a leader rather than on servanthood and service. Over and over again, I emphasize that no one should know a person is in leadership training except by the fact that he or she serves more than other people. That is the hallmark of a leader.

As we try to implement leadership training in our youth groups, we must be careful that the program does not become an end in itself. This happens when we work to keep our program going and trust our program to somehow bring people to Christ and raise up leaders. Programs usually produce managers. Relational ministry, the time you spend one-on-one showing youth your ministry or commissioning them to minister to others, most often produces leaders.

The Building Blocks of Leadership Training

After laying the foundation by understanding what leadership is and some of the advantages, limitations and dangers of leadership training with young people, we are ready to begin building a leadership training program from the ground up. I offer ten guidelines for building a leadership program into the fabric of your overall youth ministry: (1) commission all youth as ministers, (2) find youth candidates who are ready for leadership training, (3) show and tell these young persons what leadership development is all about, (4) call the young people to commitment to leadership training, (5) give them a period of basic training in servanthood, (6) involve them in the leadership training phase, the program phase and the development phase of being a Christian leader, (7) give them a ministry of their own, (8) give them opportunity to fail and to recover, (9) commission them into the process of becoming a Christian leader and (10) call them to remember what God has done for them. Let's examine these guidelines in detail.

Calling All Youth

The first guideline is very important in building a leadership training level into your youth ministry. While you are building your come level, grow level and discipleship level programs, call every young person to be a minister of Jesus. Jorge's church claims to be the church of a hundred ministers. In the same spirit, we must call our young people to go into all the world as ministers. Challenge them to be Christian leaders who are on the cutting edge of what God wants to do in the lives of other people.

In many ways, leadership training is simply helping young people to obey the Great Commission. In Bible study, Sunday school, small groups and relational teaching, we are giving young people principles to help them become Christian leaders and servants of God. We plant the seeds at the come, grow and discipleship levels that will mature into our leadership program. As young people progress to the point where they are ready to be involved in imitating the character of Christ and learning some basic skills for serving and teaching others, they are ready for hands-on experience in Christian leadership.

Finding the Potential Leaders

The second guideline is to have criteria to help you decide if a young person is ready to be involved formally in leadership training. I use the word "leader" as an acrostic for this purpose.

Led by the Spirit. Look for a young person who is led by the Spirit. Such a person is committed to a Christian lifestyle and has some measure of stability.

I'll never forget the mistake I made in this area as I

trained some young people for a mission trip to Mexico. As we went through our fifteen weeks of preparation for the trip, it became apparent that four or five of the young people in the group weren't ready. They had no consistent commitment to God. Their hearts were generally open, but their lives were not committed to Christ and serving other people. They just wanted to go to Mexico and have a good time. But I didn't have the foresight or the courage to discuss the nature and goals of our trip on a personal level and let them graciously bow out.

As we were serving in Mexico, we had some good results. Individuals were converted and we were well received by the people in the Satillo area. But the night before we were to leave, one of the local people told me that some members of our group had been overheard talking about the Mexican people in a derogatory and demeaning way. Those few words from those young people, who weren't ready to be involved in serving others in leadership ministry, went a long way toward undoing all the effort that we had put into this event. These youth were not led by the Spirit and lacked the character necessary to lead others effectively into a new relationship with God and minister to their needs.

Eager. We have got to look for young people who are eager to serve and to lead. We don't need any prima donnas. Plato said that any man who desires power is not worthy of it. Certainly, we need to find young people who aren't as interested in being up front and being noticed as they are in helping others. We need to look for young people who have matured.

Age. Early adolescence is a stormy, unsettled time. The junior high years, ages eleven to thirteen or fourteen, seem to be a little early for leadership training. Certainly, these youth need an opportunity to serve others, but when it comes to leading Bible studies or small groups, we should turn to middle and late adolescents. Usually, youth in tenth grade through college are at the prime age for involvement in a leadership training program.

Disciples. Look for young people who are disciples, who have made a solid commitment to Christ, who have learned from the Word of God and who have promised to live their lives according to God's standards. Young people need to know how to gain strength and inspiration from the community of believers. A prerequisite for leadership training is to be a disciple, a person committed to following Jesus and willing to be accountable for living a consistent Christian life at home and at school.

Eye of the tiger. You may have seen the "Rocky" movie in which Rocky was being trained to fight by Apollo Creed, his former enemy. But no matter how hard they tried, Rocky just couldn't seem to recapture that animal determination, that inward passion, that had made him a champion. The movie called this kind of inner desire the "eye of the tiger," and it was the first time I'd ever heard a name given to that invisible passion that some people have and others don't. That's the kind of passion we are looking for in our young candidates. In our eyes, they might not have the skills or the personality necessary to be a great leader, but if they have that eye of the tiger, that passionate desire for God's best, God can use them in a mighty way. They can learn what they need to learn and will be effective in serving God and others.

Real. Teenagers are in a time of great transition. Because leadership requires being in front of a group and attempting to lead them closer to God or to serve their needs, a leader is in a place of great vulnerability. James writes, "Not many of you should presume to be teachers, my brothers, because you know that we who teach will be judged more strictly" (James 3:1). James is warning us that we who attempt to lead will be judged by a high standard. The only protection we can give our young people against the times they will inevitably mess up is real honesty. This means being willing to admit, "I made a mistake, I was wrong, I failed, I was unwise. I meant to do well and I didn't. I blatantly rebelled against God and sinned and participated in something shameful to my position as a leader."

If our young people have that kind of realness, they can be the leaders that God wants them to be. We don't have to wait until young people are perfect to offer them leadership training, we just have to wait until they are real enough to admit their mistakes.

The apostle Paul gave a list of requirements for leaders in 1 Timothy 3:1-7, "Here is a trustworthy saying: If anyone sets his heart on being an overseer [a leader], he desires a noble task. Now the overseer must be above reproach, the husband of but one wife, temperate, self-controlled, respectable, hospitable, able to teach, not given to drunkenness, not violent but gentle, not quarrelsome, not a lover of money. He must manage his own family well and see that his children obey him with proper respect. (If anyone does not know how to manage his own family, how can he take care of God's church?) He must not be a recent convert, or he may become conceited and fall under the same judgment as the devil. He must also have a good reputation with outsiders, so that he will not fall into disgrace and into the devil's trap."

Although we are not by any means thrusting young people into important places of responsibility such as those Paul was discussing, we *are* training them to someday hold those positions. Therefore, we must call our youth to measure themselves by those standards if they want to become candidates for leadership training. Here is a test that I give our young people at the beginning and end of their leadership training based on the apostle Paul's requirements for Christian leaders. This tool helps youth measure their progress as they participate in the leadership program.

CHARACTER TEST—based on 1 Timothy, chapter 3

A. I have a blameless spirit.

B. I am devoted to my family.

C. I am balanced, not excessive in lifestyle.

D. I have foresight, try to think through matters, am not impulsive.

E. I am respected for my commitment to Jesus and others.

F. I am generous and pleasant to guests and visitors.

G. I am able to teach others.

H. I am loving and kind—not argumentative and combative.

I. I do not let anything control me other than God and my decision.

J. I am not harsh and cruel but patient and gentle.

K. I am in love with people and not things.

L. I manage my school work and other responsibilities efficiently and effectively.

M. I have been committed to Christ for at least three years.

N. I realize I have a desperate need for God.

O. I always make an effort to convince people that all my strength and glory comes from God.

P. Non-Christians who know me respect my faith and life.

Q. I am not two-faced, deceitful, shifty or a double-talker.

R. I do not attempt to make myself look better than I am.

S. I am willing to be tested and serve before I am chosen.

T. I do not gossip.

U. I am dependable.

V. I have a daily devotional time.

W. I attend youth meetings faithfully.

X. When people come to me with problems, I sincerely listen and try to help them.

Y. I sincerely try to be warm and open to people who are less fortunate than I am—and try to always find something good and attractive in them.

Z. I will always follow Christ.

Once you have criteria to help determine when young persons are ready for leadership training, take the list of names of people in your youth group and begin to pray for and spend time with them. You can't evaluate whether a young person is really committed to God, eager to serve, at the right age to handle leadership emotionally and mentally, has the eye of the tiger and is real and honest if you don't know him or her.

Do not rush into leadership training. One can rush into evangelism or teaching the Bible because these meet needs that everyone has. But it is vitally important that we do not rush into discipleship and leadership training. We must give God, our young people and ourselves enough time to form relationships because they are the basis of these ministries.

As you pray for and form relationships with your young people, you will see several who are ready to begin training to serve God and the group.

Time for Show and Tell

After you make your list of potential young leaders, you can begin the next step, which I call "show and tell." Take the list of young people you have selected as candidates for leadership training and invite them to be a formal or informal part of something you do. Perhaps you could have them give a testimony or read a Scripture and make some comments, or they might lead a song during a Bible study you lead. You might take them on a youth retreat you'll be leading and have them help you according to their gifts. If they are comfortable speaking, ask them to say something. If they are comfortable serving, let them help you in whatever way they can, perhaps with refreshments or recreation. Whatever you do, let the youth join you and see you doing leadership tasks. You serve the refreshments, conduct the Bible study, lead the recreation or visit an elderly person while showing and telling the young recruits what to do.

This process will help you determine whether these young people are ready for more intensive, formal leadership training. Chances are, if they frequently don't show up for things you invite them to be a part of, they aren't really ready for that kind of responsibility. But if you see in them the desire to be of value to God and others, you are probably ready to move on to the next step, which is calling them to commit to formal leadership training.

Calling Youth to Commit to Leadership Training

Since you have already been praying for these young people, and they have already joined you in some informal or formal leadership experience, you know whether to invite them to commit themselves to extensive leadership training. When making the invitation, carefully explain that you want them to commit to the first seven week program which will help them become more Christlike so that they will be better leaders. Point out that they will also learn some basic skills in communication, management and teaching so God can more effectively use them to make a better youth group, home and world. This leadership training will help them discover who they are and what their gifts are. It will give them practical experience in ministry. Try to communicate the entire vision to them. Let them know that after they experience the first seven-week session, they can then decide whether to participate in future sessions.

Basic Training—The Boot Camp Experience

Before beginning the seven-week program, which I call

Leadership Training I-VII, I try to involve future leaders in a boot camp experience. This can be done during a weekend retreat or as a stress camp. The goal of such an event is to erase the concept of leadership that the world teaches. The boot camp experience shows that leadership does not mean status or power in the sense of ruling and lording it over others. You are to free the youth from the idea that leadership means doing less work and being served by other people. After you dispel any egocentric ideas about leadership, you want to convince them that, first and foremost, leadership means servanthood. They must learn that if one wants to be a Christian leader, one must serve God and other people in Jesus' name.

Accomplishing this can be a lot of fun. You can give the youth buckets and sponges and have them wash walls or clean commodes. You can assign them group problems that force them to work with each other as a team to find solutions. You can have youth visit shut-ins. They should be doing inglorious, thankless work. Look for opportunities to challenge their perseverance and commitment. During basic training, you need to hold them strictly accountable to build character and enhance their spiritual formation. Boot camp should burn away the idea that leadership will be a lot of fun for *me* and will bring a lot of attention to *me*. Help your youth realize that leadership training involves deepening one's service and love for God and others.

Involving Youth in Leadership Training

Young people who have survived boot camp and are still interested in leadership training are ready for Leadership Training I-VII. The content of the seven units varies in different scenarios. I don't propose that you start this program if you can present these concepts relationally, which we have emphasized at various places in this book already. The important thing is not to duplicate this program, but to teach young people skills to help them discover who they are and to get them involved in a leadership experience.

We usually start our leadership program with tenth graders, but we have occasionally incorporated ninth graders into the overflow of our leadership training. We generally start our program in the fall session of the tenth grade and we coordinate our seven week session with the school semester. Our goal in Leadership I and II, which are fall and spring of the sophomore year, is primarily to convince young people that leadership equals servanthood and that without character they have no leadership.

Leadership I and II focus on character building. Each continues the discipling process by strengthening one's character, which is so vital to being a leader. Without a Christlike character one will surely fail at leadership. The foolishness of Christian leaders who have fallen into immorality and dishonesty shows that this sort of training should have been offered to many television evangelists, pastors and youth ministers. I wish someone had trained me in this area when I was a young man.

Character building is generally accomplished through character studies and discipleship. Hold youth accountable for *daily* prayer, Bible study, academic work, family

GUIDELINES FOR A

It should be:

1. carefully worded;

2. three minutes in length;

3. realistic; don't say you haven't had any problems, but rather that Christ is with you, helping you through them.

Things to avoid:

4. negative comments about the church, a particular denomination or organizations;

5. stereotypes;

6. speaking in generalities such as being a Christian is "great" or "fantastic"; be specific!

7. saying "I've been changed"; tell *how*;

8. words that are meaningless to non-Christians (Christianese: redeemed, sanctified, etc.)

Three parts:

1. Life before you were a Christian.

2. *How* you became a Christian.

3. How it has affected your life.

Things to do:

1. Try to start with an attention getting phrase.

2. Use one or two Scripture verses.

3. Write it out in advance.

4. Emphasize that *Jesus* had made all the difference in your life.

Guidelines for a person who became a Christian later in life:

1. Begin with an attention-getting sentence.

2. Before I received Christ, I lived and thought this way.

3. How I received Christ.

time and social time. Examine the lives of the great men and women of God in the Bible. What qualities of character did the great leaders of the Scriptures possess?

In Leadership I and II, we also teach some basic skills necessary for vital Christian ministry. Some of the first skills we teach are relational skills, because we are committed to the idea that God best communicates himself to people through a caring relationship. You will be a much more effective tool in God's hands if you know the person you are trying to win to Christ. So we teach the basics of how to be a good friend and how to contact people, love them and build a relationship that God can use. We teach communication skills that can help young leaders share the gospel, such as how to give a testimony (see the "Guidelines for a Personal Testimony" reprinted below). We may have youth write their testimonies and later present them in some setting where they feel comfortable. Youth

PERSONAL TESTIMONY

4. After I received Christ, these *specific changes took place in my life.*

5. Pertinent or favorite verse to close with and tie thoughts together (optional).

Guidelines for a person who accepted Christ at a young age:

1. Begin with an attention-getting sentence.

2. Background and early Christian experience (example: Went to church all my life and grew up in a Christian home).

3. Life between my early Christian experience and when I totally yielded my life to Christ.

4. How I yielded my life to Christ and specific changes that took place afterward.

5. Favorite verse (optional).

Checklist:

1. Does my testimony express the assurance that I have eternal life?

2. Have I clearly indicated how a person can receive Christ?

3. Do I have too much "travelogue" detail?

4. What positive benefits of my relationship to Christ have I mentioned?

Read the apostle Paul's testimony in Acts 26:1-29.

We also give youth spot experience in ministry in as many areas as possible in the year's time, while working behind the scenes to facilitate their ministry. We want them to gain experience in the ministry of sharing their resources and their time.

who are at ease sharing with a whole group may be asked to share one-on-one with someone on the ministry team, a church member or someone in their family.

As we explore how the goals of leadership training can be accomplished in a structured leadership training program, we emphasize again that relational leadership development is crucial within or without the structured program.

Leadership III and IV challenge teens to understand the biblical view of the various gifts, graces and personality types found in the body of Christ; discover their own personality and giftedness through a simplified personality test and a gift-discovery test found in *Discovering Your Spiritual Gifts* by Kenneth Kinghorn and provide a variety of experiences in service to others. At this level of leadership development, youth are challenged to find the flavor of ministry that is compatible with their God-given gifts, graces and personality.

Leadership V and VI focus on launching the young leaders into a ministry within the youth group, school or community. This service/ministry is their responsibility. We provide a job/ministry description (see sample job description box), accountability and encouragement. The young person (usually a senior) is urged to select a ministry in an area that fits his or her gifts and interests. Youth are involved in ministry at every level of the funnel as well as in relational ministry. This outreach creates the necessary spiritual gravitational pull that draws their peers closer to Christian discipleship.

Leadership VII focuses on short-term ministry/mission experience beyond the local church. These short-term opportunities help mature and sharpen leadership (servanthood) abilities while, at the same time, they provide a positive impact for Christ on the world. Leadership VII has a two-fold emphasis: summer missions and tithing portions of one's life to ministry.

Mission opportunities. Each summer our youth ministry offers teens two summer mission opportunities. The first is a cross-cultural ministry tour (perhaps Mexico or Alaska), and the second is a local, Kentucky mission experience. Participants must commit themselves to fifteen

Sample Job Description for a Leadership Training Project

The Big Brother/Sister ministry is a one-to-one discipling ministry aimed at stimulating growth, concentrating attention and motivating action in the lives of both the discipler and the disciplee. This ministry, more often than not, involves helping the Little Brother or Sister obtain one or more of the following:

1. clarity about their salvation (commitment to God);
2. a consistent, vital quiet time (Scripture reading and prayer);
3. a positive self-image;
4. positive-submissive relationship with parents/authorities;
5. and maintaining genuine friendships;
6. victory over sinful habits;
7. good study habits;
8. a model for—and an understanding of—real "love";
9. a commitment to and acceptance by the body of Christ;
10. motivation and instruction in loving outreach to others.

This can be accomplished by establishing weekly meetings of thirty minutes to one-and-a-half hours with the Little Brother/Sister. This meeting might follow the suggested outline below:

1. Open with prayer.
2. Discuss the week's experience (small talk) gradually moving to more serious talk.
3. Introduce the subject of discussion.
4. Study scripture that deals with subject..
5. Discuss how to apply Scripture to life (be practical and detailed).
6. Discuss what hinders the Scripture from being applied.
7. Set up practical steps for overcoming.
8. Give assignment.
9. Take prayer requests and pray.
10. Encourage and remind youth of next week's time.

This is *only* a guide. You should find and/or develop your own materials, methods, meeting times and places (in conjunction with the youth director).

Remember: above all, you are there to help serve your Little Brother/Sister!

to twenty weeks of discipleship/leadership training (character building, culture/language studies and ministry preparation). Our goals for these tours include:

(1) to build in the teens a strong, disciplined relationship with God and with others;

(2) to instill a vision for Christian leadership (service) and for world-impacting outreach;

(3) to provide training in basic leadership skills (speaking, administration, construction, prayer, etc.);

(4) to facilitate hands-on experience in ministry; and

(5) to offer practical help/ministry to a hurting world.

Tithing One's Life. Leadership VII challenges youth to give a portion of their lives (one month to two years) to Christian ministry. The Church of the Latter Day Saints of Jesus Christ (the Mormons) have had tremendous growth largely due to the fact that most of their youth devote two years to missionary service. Uncle Sam also requires this service from our youth in times of national crisis. How much more we should call for our youth to consider tithing a portion of their lives for the kingdom of God! (This challenge, however, should never become the standard of orthodoxy, the mark for real disciples.) I am convinced we in mainline denominations need to challenge our youth to Christian heroism in service to a world in dire need.

In leadership development we complete the cycle of Scripture's command to grow, disciple and reproduce. The benefit and growth that result from committed youth giving themselves in ministry to their peers is powerful and exciting. Truly, leadership training is engaged in the struggle for the hearts and minds of youth. And our churches, communities and nation hang in the balance of this struggle's outcome. Will the twenty-first century be lead by the "isms" of the world or by Christ Jesus? I propose that Christian youth ministry can help answer that question locally and nationally.

8 *Relational Ministry*

One-on-One Approach Is Ministry on the Cutting Edge

By Jorge Acevedo

A busy executive ran through the double doors into the train station, leaving behind him the pressures of his job. His only thought was his beautiful, warm family. He dreamed of playing with his children and could almost taste his wife's good cooking. He had to hurry to catch the train out of the city to the suburbs, so he ran down the station's long, crowded corridors. As he turned the corner onto the final stretch to his homebound train, he did not see a little boy who was squatting down, playing with some marbles. The running executive ran into the boy and the marbles flew everywhere. But the man kept running, thinking, "If I stop, I'll miss my train, my time with my family, my dinner!" A few steps later, however, he stopped. He walked back to the boy and helped him gather the marbles. Amazed, the little boy looked into the man's face and asked, "Mister, are you Jesus?"

At the heart of youth ministry is a desire to point youth to God by being the hands and feet of Jesus. This chapter explores the meaning and methods of a relational approach to youth ministry. We'll examine a ministry of presence; some approaches to youth ministry; the benefits, dangers and character of relational ministry; and practical techniques for implementing a relational approach to youth ministry. In this chapter, we'll also note the several advantages and disadvantages of relational ministry and programmatic ministry.

I would hope that pulsating through every chapter of this book is the fact that relational ministry should always be the foot we step forward with first. Relational ministry is the essence, the substance, of effective youth ministry. Program provides the context or skeleton of ministry.

A Ministry of Presence

The truth the New Testament screams the loudest is that God became man in the person of Jesus Christ (John 1:1-18). The "incarnation" was God becoming flesh, a human being, a man. Ultimately, Jesus' death, burial and resurrection are God's expression of love for us.

Jesus' life and ministry show us the essential nature of a ministry of presence, or relational ministry. When he sent his Son, God quit merely speaking to Israel through prophets, priests and kings. Jesus models for us God's approach to ministry, an approach that seeks to be a real presence to people in their culture.

In his earthly ministry, Jesus never established a program for his disciples. Instead, he spent time with the crowds, the twelve and the three (Peter, James and John). His relationship with individuals changed them—not some "heavenly" program.

In 1 Thessalonians 2, Paul tells the Christians in Thessalonica how, as the founding father of the church there, he came with gentleness and boldness to preach the gospel that had been entrusted to him as an apostle. Using the image of a nursing mother, in verses 7-8 Paul tells of his affection for them:

". . . we were gentle among you, like a mother caring for her little children. We loved you so much that we were delighted to share with you not only the gospel of God but our lives as well, because you had become so dear to us."

The image is clear. Paul invested in the believers not only the good news of Jesus, but also his life. Both Paul's preaching about salvation through Jesus and his real, human presence helped establish the church at Thessalonica.

Other passages that support the solid scriptural basis for relational ministry include Luke 5:27-31, Luke 15:1-2, Mark 10:45, Philippians 2:5-8, 1 Thessalonians 1:5-6, 1 Corinthians 2:1-5 and 2 Corinthians 5:20.

Throughout the Word of God, from Adam to the apostle John, relational ministry was always at the forefront of what God was doing. God related to people, called men and women to relate to each other in the body of Christ and called the body of Christ to relate to the greater community.

God's approach to ministry has rarely been programmatic. Even the Old Testament days of ritualistic sacrifices in the Temple were, as Hebrews 7-10 explain, just shadows of what God planned to reveal in the person of Jesus Christ.

We youth ministers need to understand and imitate the biblical example of a ministry of presence. Our lives are the medium through which young people can best hear the life-changing message of Jesus Christ. We will see God do incredible things when we commit ourselves to being a presence in their lives.

Youth Ministry Approaches—Which Does Your Church Use?

Two basic approaches to youth ministry are: (1) a church focus model and (2) a cultural focus model. The church focus model establishes a program and then calls youth to join the program. This is how many churches do youth ministry. Adults meet together, plan a program, invite youth and have the event. This approach is also, for the most part, generic. It cannot "target" an individual and seek to meet his or her specific needs.

Advantages of this church-focused, programmatic ministry are that it is much more stable than relational or culturally-focused ministries. It can be relied upon. It is objective. It is not as dependent on people and personalities. It is predictable. It is safe. It gives a sense of security, tradition, strength and realness to ministry. It can be measured and evaluated in terms of one's goals in ministry, the numbers of youth who participate and the amount of money spent to run the program. It is much easier to define and to implement than the cultural focus model.

However, a program can become form without substance. It can have the form of godliness but deny the power of God (which is one of Paul's concerns and predictions about the last days). Certainly, many mainline churches demonstrate how our programs can be right in precept and doctrine but very dead in relational dynamics and effectiveness in meeting people's needs and bringing them to God.

Programs have a way of becoming a sacred cow. People's needs are dynamic; times change, culture changes and perspectives change. But programs don't tend to change at all. If they do change, they change much more slowly than the dynamic trends happening in the lives of people and cultures.

On the other hand, the cultural focus model seeks to meet youth in their own culture. It attempts to bring the gospel to them, instead of bringing them to the gospel. This approach uses personal relationships as avenues for ministry. Like Jesus, who left the safety of heaven, youth workers must leave the safety of the church. By entering into the world of the adolescent, the youth worker can better meet the needs of teenagers.

The cultural focus model works. I remember one church I served which used a church-focus model. The youth program there involved only about twenty youth in a church of eight hundred members. My instincts led me to revamp the youth program to minister to youth within their culture. This relational approach immediately paid big dividends. Within a year, the number of active youth had doubled and, more importantly, the group gained a spiritual dimension that had been missing.

Relational ministry is culturally relevant. To do relational ministry, you must enter into young people's culture and minister to them exactly the same way you would enter into the culture of some national group in another country.

The difference between the two models is essentially the contrast between a programmatic and a relational approach to youth ministry.

Therefore we contend that the heart of youth ministry is building friendships with teenagers to win them to Christ (come level), teaching them God's ways (grow level), helping them develop Christian lifestyles (discipleship level), and raising them up to be leaders in the Church of Jesus Christ (leadership level). Relational ministry is the principle that makes the funnel illustration (chapter three) work.

At the come level, relational ministry is one of the most powerful ways to call young people to come to God because we enter into their culture by attending ball games, plays and things that interest them, in places where youth who do not attend church congregate. In relational ministry, we go to the hedges, highways and byways and call young people to come. We become the voices of God. We do not remain cloistered inside the Temple calling, "come in, come in." Instead, we go out to where the young people live and minister to them. This is one of the most thrilling things we can do.

At the grow level, we really get to know young people. As we find out what interests them and spend time with them, we earn the right to be heard. We share Jesus with them; if they come to God, great. If they do not, we continue showing them the unconditional love of God even though they claim they are not interested. But the young people who *have* committed their lives to Christ need to grow. They need to understand the relevance of God's Word to their daily lives. Through contact ministry, we share with them as their needs unfold. We can address their needs very specifically and precisely—whether it be the need to grasp the principles of God's Word, the need for fellowship and support or the need for accountability—at the exact time such help is needed and when the young person shows interest. This is more effective than trying to arouse such interest through programmatic machinations.

The relational approach is also vital during discipleship and leadership training. As we teach, work, play and cry with young people, we learn their hungers and frustrations as they want to become the persons that God has called them to be. We can adapt our ministry to these evolving situations. How beautifully relational ministry synchronizes with their interests, passions and abilities.

Benefits of Relational Ministry

Keeping in Touch with Specific Needs

Youth live in a constant state of flux. Their lives change as quickly as the clock moves. A relational approach to ministry allows you to be in touch with the specific needs of individual youth in your group as well as with your group as a whole. A programmatic approach cannot address these rapidly changing individual needs.

Cindy (not her real name) looked depressed as the senior highs gathered in the youth basement before Sunday school. Taking her aside, I asked her if she were okay. She asked me if we could talk in my office. As I closed the door, she began to cry. For the next hour, she told me how she had intercourse with her boyfriend the week before and was feeling guilty. We talked and prayed together. My relational approach to ministry, which meant spending time with Cindy, became the avenue for significant healing. A programmatic approach would simply schedule a sex education class every so often and would miss any individual needs.

Programmatic ministry is designed for a group of people and, therefore, must be generic. Because it deals with more than one person's needs, culture, experience and personality, it becomes bland and general.

It is also very easy for a program to become an end in itself. We slip into the habit of presenting the program and expecting young people to come so that the program can continue. We even begin to put people on guilt trips, saying they ought to be involved in the program and should attend meetings because it is the right thing to do, regardless of the program's effectiveness or value. The program can distract from and become a barrier to God's reaching people, thus destroying what ministry is all about.

Winning the Right to Be Heard

Youth ministers who practice relational ministry seek to develop genuine friendships with teenagers. As the friendship between youth and adult deepens and trust increases, significant ministry can take place. In contrast, a programmatic approach rarely asks the question, "Have I won the right to be heard?" Relational ministry focuses on building relationships and raising trust levels as avenues for presenting the life-changing claims of Jesus Christ.

While serving in inner-city Dallas, Hule met a young, desperate alcoholic in our neighborhood who was living out of the trash bins at a McDonald's restaurant. Because he ministered to this man's food, housing, vocational and financial needs, the man began to trust Hule to minister to his spiritual and emotional needs as well. Soon, Hule's visits to the man's run-down crash pad led to relational contact with many other needy people. Hule had won the right to be heard and was able to respond in a Christian manner.

Building a Foundation for Discipline

During a youth leader's seminar, one of the most frequently asked questions is "How do I discipline my kids?" Youth workers struggle to balance love and order. On the one hand, they want to create an environment that is characterized by grace and acceptance. On the other hand, they want to be firm and maintain order.

A relational approach to ministry solves this dilemma by winning the right to discipline. The more time you spend with a young person, the more respect that youth will have for you and your program.

For example, Jim, an angry, street-tough youth, was a consistent discipline problem. His unreasoning anger and defiance kept him on the verge of being expelled from school. However, I rarely had any discipline problems with him, even during a military-style stress camp. Why? Because I spent time with Jim once a week at lunch and during hunting and fishing expeditions, Jim knew I loved him. Thus, he respected our youth group's rules and even obeyed when he was angry.

Personalizing Ministry

A teenager's life is like a roller coaster. One minute, he's up. The next minute, he's down. A relational ministry moves with the ebb and flow of a youth's changing life. It seeks to minister to a youth's needs where he or she is at that moment. In contrast, a programmatic ministry is rigid, not fluid. The best a program can do is meet the needs of a few within a group. In their search for adult identity and their pilgrimage to own their faith, many youth resist going to church programs.

Billy, for example, was not interested in joining our (in his view) phoney, hypocritical youth program. But rather than marking his name off our list as a spiritual casualty, I sought to do something with Bill (in his case, hunt or fish) every two weeks. Often we spoke at length about his doubt, anger and fear. Through this relational touch, Bill has remained in the orbit of the church and has made significant spiritual steps.

Relational ministry moves with the young person's ups and downs. It ministers to his needs, rushes when he is ready to rush and slows when he slows. It is as dynamic as the life of teenagers.

Relational ministry is also very flexible. It adapts to the over-commitment and busyness of our culture. It can minister to a young person at breakfast before the day gets started or after the ball game on Friday night.

Encouraging Leadership

Relational ministry enhances a person's leadership qualities. The activity of reaching out, finding out where young people are, serving them, and moving them toward God has a way of keeping one in touch with the people to whom you minister. It also inspires honest and effective leadership. A programmatic focus, on the other hand, has a way of producing managers whose focus is not necessarily the people but the program. These managers set goals and implement programs to help people be loyal to and to be involved with the program, not Christ.

A Defense of Programs

Are we proposing that youth ministers abandon programs for pure, undefiled relational ministry? No, never in a thousand years! Just as the body needs the skeleton and the skeleton needs the body, so we need programs to give context and longevity to our ministry. Programs give youth parameters that they can recognize.

However, if we offer programs devoid of the relational touch, without entering into youths' lives, we have a flesh-less skeleton that is cold and impersonal and very empty. But when we add the relational component to the skeleton, we flesh it out with life-giving, vital ministry that gives young people a sense of personhood.

Relational ministry tells young persons that they are important, that God's attention is on them, that he understands their feelings and that he meets them where they are in genuine love and concern.

Dangers of Relational Ministry

Any task worth doing involves risk. Attempting to be a significant adult in the lives of young people is no exception. Knowing some of the dangers of this style of ministry can help you avoid some traps.

Being Misunderstood

Frank was a terrific youth worker. He loved youth, and his youth group was growing in numbers as well as spiritually. But when he underwent his bi-annual staff review, the chairperson of the Staff-Relations Committee asked Frank why he spent so much time with kids instead of being in his office. Frank was floored! He felt that he was being grossly misunderstood. The reason he spent time with youth was to build a better youth group; yet now he had to explain why he played basketball with the guys and went to the mall with the girls.

As Frank had discovered, being misunderstood is one of the dangers of a youth ministry that seeks to build relationships with teenagers. Such a youth minister may be labeled lazy or immature.

One way to short-circuit this problem is to let the church know up front that this is your style of ministry. My friend Bill Hughes at First United Methodist Church in Lexington, Kentucky, let his church know he intended to use the relational method of building a youth group. The church responded by establishing an expense account for him to use as he ministers to teenagers. Clearly, explaining your intention can lessen the danger of being misunderstood.

Losing Your Adult Identity

One of the greatest dangers of relational ministry is losing one's identity as an adult. It's easy to become "just one of the guys" as you relate with your youth. If this happens, the youth worker has lost his or her role as an authority and cannot be a significant adult in a youth's life. Being a friend to teenagers without becoming like an adolescent friend is a tightrope we must walk with extreme care.

As you seek to identify with youth, remember that they want an adult role model or "significant other" with whom to relate. To avoid becoming an overgrown teenager, ask yourself the question "Why am I acting this way?" If the answer is just to have fun with a youth and build a relationship, then everything is fine. If, though, you are "needing" acceptance and want "just to be liked" by the youth, you have stepped over the line.

Playing Favorites

Remember the child who was the "teacher's pet" in grade school? Everybody hated that person. For some reason, nobody likes a person who has the inside track on things or gets "perks" for being the favorite. The same is true in youth ministry. It's easy to play favorites with a few youth, especially those who give you lots of personal affirmation, but you must guard against spending excessive time with only a few youth. Spread around the gravy of your attention.

One way to avoid playing favorites, as well as some of the other dangers of relational ministry, is to share the ministry with others. This does at least two things. It keeps you accountable to a group of other adults, and it helps others carry the load of relational ministry (note chapter eleven on team ministry).

Sexual Temptations

Spending time with youth of the opposite sex can be

dangerous, and more and more ministers are failing in this area. Many youth workers are being both falsely and accurately accused of sexual misconduct with their youth. Temptation does not respect age, sex or marital status.

Building intimate relationships with young people of the opposite sex can easily be misinterpreted by one or both parties. In 1 Thessalonians 4:1-8, Paul calls all Christians to sanctification specifically within the area of our sexual relationships. Those of us who work with teenagers need to heed these words.

Always remember that none of us are beyond temptation. "But by the grace of God, there go I" is our motto. Also, do not be naive. If a youth is getting "too close," nip it in the bud. Address the issue. Do not run from it, because it can catch up with you if it is ignored.

Measuring the Wind

Another disadvantage of relational ministry is that it is difficult to measure. In relational ministry it is tough to say with certainty whether you have made any progress with a young person because the process is slow. It emerges and evolves as your relationship and the young person's relationships with God and family and others develop.

Becoming a Personality Cult

Relational ministry's greatest disadvantage is that it can easily become a personality cult. It lends itself to being the exclusive province of extroverts who can easily contact others, build relationships and move fluently in and out of different social circles. But this need not be so. The effectiveness of this approach to ministry does not depend upon the personality of the leader.

Two Essential Characteristics of Relational Ministry

What does a youth worker who is committed to relational youth ministry look like? What are his or her characteristics? Let's examine two of the essential ingredients of a person who seeks to build relationships with teenagers.

Vulnerability

Reaching out to a youth is risky. Seeking to build a relationship means being vulnerable enough to be hurt by the youth. Although you may invest many hours in a young person, he or she still might reject you and your Lord. A well-known American youth leader once told me that he invested a year in a young man only to discover that the youth was robbing his home! Sometimes you will reach out to a teenager who does not want anything to do with you, the church or God. Realize from the beginning that relational ministry is "risky business."

I recall spending many hours with a young man in our group who liked me and the youth group, but did not want anything to do with God. For three years, I tried to point him to Jesus. He eventually left the church and today is involved in the drug culture.

We must take a risk when we give of ourselves to young people, for this is our calling and our mission. Only God knows what seeds of faith may be planted by our meager attempts to share Jesus.

Trustworthiness

Wise Solomon said in Proverbs 20:6, "Many a man claims to have unfailing love, but a faithful man who can find?" Many folks claim to be loyal, but a man or woman of trustworthiness is a premium find. As you minister to young people, be a loyal and trustworthy friend. Keeping information confidential is essential to maintaining a loyal friendship.

While I served at Trinity Hill, one of the sophomore girls in our group came to me complaining about the attitude of two guys in the group. We talked about the legitimacy of her complaint and agreed that I would talk to the young men about their attitudes. Later, I told one of our ministry team members about the situation. By doing so, I had broken her confidence. She had trusted me with private information, and I had let it leak out. She found out, and it took me over a year and a half to regain her confidence. She suffered spiritually and relationally. I share this painful story to illustrate the importance of being trustworthy in relationships with youth.

Practical Approaches to Relational Ministry

So, you may be wondering, how do I make relational ministry work in the "real world"? Following are some suggestions of ways to "become Jesus" for your youth. This is not an exhaustive list, only a few examples of ways to develop a relational ministry.

The Home Visit

Traditionally, we think of the pastor as the person who visits in the homes of church members and constituents. But it pays big dividends when we youth workers also get inside the homes of our young people and meet their parents and siblings. I have found parents to be very receptive to my presence in their homes. Also, getting to know a youth's home environment provides valuable information for further dialogue.

Counselors are telling us that a "systems" understanding of a person can give us keen insight into that individual's problems. An adolescent's most essential system is the family. As youth workers, visiting a youth's home can give us insight into family customs, rules and power structures. This understanding can help you relate personal faith in Jesus Christ to a teenager's everyday home life.

A friend of mine asked a discipleship group of senior high youth what advice he should give seminarians in an evangelism class. One response was classic. A young lady said, "Tell them to visit us in our homes. Tell them they need to know about where we live, what our parents are like, and how we interact with our brothers and sisters." Almost without a exception, the young people I visit welcome me warmly.

One of my rules of home visitation is to call before going. I very seldom just show up. I always state my intention when visiting as well. I will say, "Steve, I wanted to stop by to spend some time with you so I can get to know you better." If Steve is a new contact, I will be honest about my desire to see him get involved in our youth group. I will tell him about our activities and try to find out if he knows anybody who is active in our group. Often such a common denominator facilitates further dialogue.

In an attempt to be sensitive to the Holy Spirit and the needs of the youth, I do not push spiritual issues too quickly. My role as a Christian youth worker is a witness in and of itself. The "God-talk" will develop naturally as the relationship progresses.

Recently, I was visiting with a young man in his home. John was athletic, and as we talked he asked me about my athletic involvement. This was our first meeting, but already the conversation was flowing. I told John how my athletic career was sidelined in the tenth grade by a knee injury and how that first major setback in my life helped lead me to committing my life to Jesus. John listened intently. The conversation had moved to spiritual things, but it was a natural progression.

Whether talking with young people in their homes, at church or at fast-food restaurants, be sensitive to the leading of the Holy Spirit and to the needs of the teenager. Let the spiritual talk happen spontaneously.

The After School Get Together

For youth workers whose schedules permit, picking up youth after school is an excellent way to spend time with them and their friends. Most young people do not have as much to do from three to five in the afternoon as they do at other times. Even though some youth are very busy with after-school clubs and activities, many are readily available during this time slot. Take advantage of it!

Again, never show up without a scheduled appointment with a youth. Youth workers need to respect each young person's space. In relational ministry, we tread on their turf, so we must never invade it. Wait until you are invited to enter. This means that I do not just show up at the high school parking lot, wait until I see one of my youth and then approach that person.

After you pick up the youth take him or her to a neutral public place like a fast food restaurant or a park. The idea is to earn the right to be heard and develop a genuine relationship by your presence. Spend time asking questions and sharing about yourself. This simple, cost-effective approach to meeting with youth will have more impact than a multitude of experience programs.

School and Special Events

I was once invited to see one of our junior high girls play basketball. I paid $1.50 to get in and spent about two hours at the ball game. Within that time, I talked with ten youth, four parents and two college students from our church. The money and time invested were relatively low, but the payoff was astronomical.

In the fall, I spend most Friday nights at high school football games. I always go with a few of our youth. There I meet even more of our church's youth and their friends. I see the football players and band members from our church. I run into their parents. I meet new youth.

Attending school events makes you a presence in the lives of your youth, their friends and their parents. This makes a strong positive statement about your commitment and availability to youth and families.

Graduations, recitals, plays and talent shows are also special events to the youth in your church. They are opportunities for you to say that you care about their total lives, that they are more than just a name on a membership list. As your concern for them moves beyond the church walls into their everyday lives, you demonstrate the all-encompassing nature of the spiritual life.

At graduation time, I visit the homes of our seniors on the morning before graduation. I buy them a gift from a Christian bookstore and give the girls a single red rose. I give each graduate a card with a personalized note. All of these things are done to express my long-term commitment to them as Christians.

Hobbies and Sports

Whether your youth love to fish, hike, hunt or play basketball or soccer, you can join them in their hobbies and sports. Participating in these activities conveys your commitment to be a real presence in their lives. Find out what they like to do and go do it with them!

Very few weeks pass in which I do not meet with one guy or a group of the fellows in my youth group to play basketball. These are often the very committed Christians in the group. Our time together facilitates talk about their lives and faith. Hule Goddard is constantly hunting or fishing with guys from his youth group in Wilmore. Such times spent sharing a sport or hobby are awesome opportunities to get to know youth and to reaffirm your interest in them as individuals.

Summing Up Relational Ministry

As youth workers, our task is one of the most sacred and special in the body of Christ. God grants us the privilege of taking the hands of precious youth and walking with them to God.

In *The Blessing*, Gary Smalley and John Trent tell a beautiful story.[1] A four-year old girl became frightened during a loud thunderstorm. One loud clap of thunder sent the girl out of her bed, down the hall and into her parents' room. With a big jump, she landed right between her mother and father. Her daddy wrapped his arms around his little girl and said, "Don't worry, Honey. The Lord will protect you." The girl snuggled closer to her daddy and replied, "I know that, Daddy, but right now I need someone with skin on!" Our task as youth workers is to be someone with skin on who can walk with young people on their pilgrimages to God. It is a holy task, one we must do with prayer and gentleness.

One of the most powerful testimonies that I have seen to the significance of relational ministry is this letter from a Ph.D. to his former youth minister, Art Erickson.

Dear Art and Kathy,

I have planned this kind of letter for a number of years now . . . when I think back into my childhood and adolescence where most of my personality and spiritual growth took place, it was Art Erickson who occupied a real important place in that time of my life. I have felt it a special treat to have gotten to know Kathy these last few years, and she seems like icing on the cake to a relationship that has been with me so long in the person of Art.

When I think about what Art Erickson means to me,

it is a bit hard—similar to what I would say if asked what my mother or father or some other key figure in life would mean to me. Art Erickson in many ways for me is one of those "symbolic" persons that we each have—who emotionally almost become larger than life because of the depth of what they mean to us and the specific times in our lives that they have affected us.

I met Art when I was ten years old. I've known him for twenty years—two thirds of my life. I went on canoe trips with him, slept in tents with him, climbed mountains with him, saw his anger, his pain, his laughter, his joy. I saw him get mad at kids who deserved his anger, and then laugh with them when I wondered why he would forgive them. I saw Art living in emotional crucibles, wondering where he got the strength to continue reaching out when he was hurting so much inside. Art has been someone I idolized, someone I respected, someone I rebelled against, someone I eventually tried to understand in terms of what his life has meant.

In psychology, we have a term called "introject." An introject is someone whom we have emotionally and symbolically "taken into" our own personality. An introject is an "interior person," who in many ways is always with us, who silently looks over our shoulder as we go through life, who criticizes or praises us, who loves or scolds us. An introject becomes a part of the very depth of who we are emotionally, and in that way affects us more deeply than any books, sermons or speeches could ever affect us. Art Erickson is one of my introjects. He is an introject who has been faithful; he is an introject who has steadily cared; he is an introject who has become an interior measuring stick for the most important things in my life; above all, he is an introject in my life of Jesus Christ.

Art Erickson is a guy who never slept in the "counselors' tent." Those of you who have worked with kids know well the full meaning of that phrase. The "counselors' tent" is the place where the grown-ups went to get away from the kids—where they went to recoup their sanity and emotional balance after a long day spent with us. Where they went to shut us out and talk grown-up talk with each other, play cards and have a good time. I always felt a little lonely when the counselors were in their tent. But Art Erickson never slept there. I often wondered about that—curious that this particular grown-up always ended up with "us"—that he for some odd reason decided he liked the noise, the mold, the smelly socks that were in our tent more than the comraderie, adultness and quiet cleanness that resided in the "counselors' tent." I had a hunch that down inside he might really enjoy getting away. But for some odd reason he didn't.

He was there in our tent when I was twelve, talking with us about girls, sex and what real love was like, when other grown-ups thought we didn't care about that stuff at that age. He was there in our tent when I was thirteen and had just become a Christian and was somewhat awkwardly putting on the "new clothes" of a relationship with Christ. He was there, in a tent in Cincinnati, when I was fifteen and struggled with painful and awkward feelings about whether I was lovable or not.

He was there, in our tent when I was eighteen and out on the Colorado desert in the middle of nowhere, when we were all too tired from a day of walking twenty miles to care much about anything. He was there when I was twenty and inwardly confused and fed up with my role as a "Good Christian"; when I smashed the window of a car with a water balloon as an expression of my unrecognizable anguish inside. Art stayed in my tent through all of that stuff.

I often wondered about that habit he had, of sleeping in our tent, even though the stuff in there wasn't that pretty, neat or clean. I guess I know that I have something emotionally and spiritually from his being in my tent that I will cherish the rest of my life. Thanks Art, for caring and being there in that place for me.

With love and deep respect,
Greg

The Gospels tell a beautiful story of how Jesus, God with

skin on, practiced relational ministry. Relational ministry takes an individual or personal approach. As you get to know a young person, you can assess needs which are unique and specific to him or her. You can then fashion a ministry that will fit them perfectly, one that will address their situation precisely.

Tending the Inner Fire

Spiritual Formation and the Youth Minister

By Hule Goddard

Whether you are a youth minister entering a parish, have volunteered for youth ministry in your local church or have become a pastor whose responsibilities include youth ministry, the following seven steps can help you build an effective youth ministry from the ground up.

1. In your own spiritual formation, establish Christ as the central priority of your life, whether you are at home or in ministry. Draw the strength, the insight and the perspective you need for ministry from God, his Word and the people of God.

2. Establish your family as your first priority after God. Schedule your time so that your family complements your ministry rather than being a hindrance to it or something you neglect when you minister to others (see chapter ten).

3. When you enter a church, establish effective come and grow level programs (see chapters four and five). These provide a context in which ministry can be done.

4. Build a ministry team. Find, recruit and train people who can help you in both relational and programmatic ministry (see chapter eleven).

5. Establish a strong relational ministry, which, as

we mentioned in chapter eight, is the heart of biblical youth ministry. Make contact with every young person in your youth group and community, reaching as many as is practically possible.

6. Build an effective discipleship program to guide young people who are ready, know the principles of God's Word and want to actually do God's Word (see chapter six). This creates a community of faith in which youth help and hold each other accountable to be men and women of God.

7. Last, raise up world-changing leaders (see chapter seven) who will return to your youth program, community and schools and make a difference for Christ—young people who will reproduce themselves by leading others to Christ.

In this chapter, we focus on that first step—spiritual formation.

Most youth ministers readily acknowledge the necessity of maintaining a strong and stable spiritual life. However, the schedules, problems, programs and incessant activities leave many teen workers with, at best, unsatisfactory vertical relationships with God and his Word. The disciplines of grace so essential for balance, motivation and perspective are squeezed out by the tyranny of the urgent matters of ministry.

The Holy Spirit is the applicator of God's creative, prevenient, converting and sanctifying grace.[1] Since God first created man and woman in his image, breathing "life" and creating a "living soul," the faithful have recognized the need to nurture, develop and understand humanity's spiritual dimension, (our vertical relationship with God). Spiritual formation has been the wellspring of effective, orthodox, life-changing ministry throughout Scripture and history.

In Ecclesiastes 1:9, Solomon acknowledges, "there is nothing new under the sun." I confess that at the thirty-three year mark in my pilgrimage through life, I realize that my chances of discovering "new truth" about God, family, prayer, life and spiritual formation are slim. However, I have a great zeal to discover "fresh truth"—fresh, specialized approaches and practices to implement the wisdom of the ages.

In this spirit, this chapter will attempt to explore spiritual formation in the life of the youth minister using current biblical and historical understanding; to relate spiritual formation to the needs, struggles and cultural environment of the youth minister; and to suggest some practical spiritual disciplines that can help youth ministers grow in their relationships with God.

Abiding in the Vine

Scripture boldly documents God's involvement in man's spiritual formation. God the Father created man "a little lower" than himself (see Psalm 8:5) and crowned us with his own image. God the Son then gave us life a second time through redemption from sin's death (Ephesians 2:1-8). And God the Holy Spirit nurtures our daily growth in grace (1 Corinthians 3:7).

Jesus told his disciples "I am the true vine, and my Father is the gardener. . . . Remain in me and I will remain in you. No branch can bear fruit by itself; it must remain in the vine. Neither can you bear fruit, unless you remain in me" (John 15:1, 4). Disciples then and throughout history have rarely doubted the sufficiency and richness of the vine (God's role in spiritual formation). Rather, they have questioned our ability to "remain" (mankind's role in spiritual formation). Gordon McDonald admits, "It has not been a simple thing for me to perceive the process and the purposes by which Christ wants to 'abide' in my private world."[2] This quest, with its resultant understandings and disciplines, is what is known as spiritual formation.

Man's odyssey to develop a vital union with God is vividly recorded in Scripture and church history. Here are some examples:

■ Abraham prayed, covenanted and sacrificed to God (Genesis 17).
■ Moses experienced solitude, worship, prayer and service (Exodus 2-10).
■ Caleb and Joshua fully obeyed and courageously served (Numbers 14).

■ Samuel faithfully worshiped and gave guidance (1 Samuel 12).

■ David confessed, worshiped and meditated (Psalm 1, 51, 92).

■ Jehoshaphat fasted and sought guidance (2 Chronicles 20).

■ Isaiah confessed, worshiped and submitted (Isaiah 6).

■ Daniel prayed, studied and served (Daniel 6-10).

■ Nehemiah prayed, served and celebrated (Nehemiah 1-9).

■ John the Baptist sought solitude, silence and simplicity (Luke 3).

■ Jesus sought solitude, prayed, served and worshiped (the Gospels).

■ The apostles prayed in one accord and fasted (Acts 2, 13).

■ Paul prayed, served and celebrated (Acts 9-28; Philippians 4).

■ Peter wept bitterly over his sin and served (Luke 22 and Acts 1-8).

■ John meditated, prayed and celebrated (Revelation 6-22).

■ Origen championed prayer and study.[3]
■ St. Anthony explored solitude.[4]
■ St. Augustine studied, confessed and celebrated.[5]
■ St. Francis of Assisi championed simplicity.
■ St. Teresa of Avila exhausted herself in prayer and meditation.[6]
■ John Wesley prayed, studied and served.[7]
■ Francis Asbury personified service.[8]
■ Charles Finney prayed, fasted and served.[9]
■ Thomas Merton revived meditation.[10]
■ Henri Nouwen revived solitude and silence.[11]
■ Richard Foster celebrated the disciplines.[12]

These experiences of the saints of the ages reveal several methods for effectively remaining in the vine. These methods, commonly called classical disciplines, include prayer, confession, sacraments, worship, meditation, fast-ing, study, simplicity, solitude, submission, service, guidance and celebration.[13]

As Foster explains, "They are not classical merely because they are ancient, although they have been practiced by sincere people over the centuries. The Disciplines are classical because they are *central* to experiential Christianity. In one form or another all of the devotional masters have affirmed the necessity of the Disciplines."[14]

This great cloud of witnesses makes it awesomely clear to us that any Christian, and especially those called to the ministry, must give utmost attention to this business of spiritual formation.

Do You Have What It Takes?

In 1 Timothy 3:1-7, the apostle Paul outlines the qualifications for a minister (or "overseer"):

1. A minister must be committed in his or her intent to love God and others—free of blatant, intentional sin—*blameless.*

2. A minister must be balanced and in control of his or her life's schedule—full of zeal, yet paced to last a lifetime—growing spiritually, emotionally, physically—*temperate.*

3. A minister must have foresight and plan ahead to maximize ministry opportunities and to minimize problems and distractions—*prudent.*

4. A minister must be radically committed to integrity and genuinely in love with Jesus and others (free of phoniness)—*respectable.*

5. A minister must be open, warm and accepting of all people regardless of their social status, emotional stability, need or sin—*hospitable.*

6. A minister must be able to teach life-giving principles of Scripture through adequate study, planning and obedience—*able to teach.*

7. A minister must not be controlled by passions and appetites, and not be overindulgent—*not pugnacious.*

8. A minister must not derive security, self-image, prestige or power from money—financial considerations should not become paramount in deciding career moves—*free from the love of money.*

9. A minister must be caring, loving, gentle; never harsh, defensive or argumentative—*gentle, uncontentious.*

10. A minister must be in control of his or her own life and family—committed to fostering the spiritual, emotional, fiscal and physical needs of that family— and committed to a schedule that reflects God's priorities—*manage first his own household well.*

11. A minister must not become obsessed with his or her professional career and past laurels, and must not serve God out of selfish ambition—*not a new convert lest he become conceited and fall into the condemnation of the devil.*

12. A minister must earn the right to be heard by maintaining, through thick and thin, a lifestyle that reflects commitment, love and devotion for God and others—*have a good reputation.*

The only hope any child of Adam whom God has called to ministry has of qualifying biblically as an overseer is "the way of disciplined grace."[15] Only God's grace at work in us can produce, in growing degrees, blamelessness, temperance, prudence, etc. Only consistent practice of the classical disciplines can bring us to the point where God can do something through us. The disciplines are "God's means of grace."[16] Thus, God's call to ministry includes God's call to an exemplary life of daily, consistent involvement in spiritual formation.

Spiritual Formation in the Real World of Youth Ministry

The field of youth ministry has seen refreshing growth as more and more people consider ministry to adolescents a profession. Unfortunately, youth ministers' spiritual formation and training have not developed at the same pace as the expanding job opportunities and demands of the church's burgeoning youth programs. Thus, under-trained or untrained youth ministers (often in late adolescence themselves at age twenty to twenty four) who may still be struggling with their own self-identity and maturity, are called to serve.[17] Such ministers face at least three enormous challenges: the low-rated, high-paced nature of youth ministry; parental expectations; and the suspiciousness, inconsistency and narcissism of contemporary youth.

High Expectations—No Respect. As Noel Becchetti observes, "The average length of service for a church youth worker is still around eighteen months. Something is not right."[18] The church's view of youth ministry has been frustratingly utilitarian. The laity and clergy want quality counseling, teaching, disciplining and programming for youth, yet continue to view the youth minister as a probationary preacher-intern on the way to becoming a "real" minister. Many people view youth ministry as a mere stepping stone to future ministry to adults.

Parents Should Be Partners, But. . . Adolescence is a stormy time for parents and their children. In their fear and frustration, parents look to the youth minister to "fix in one year what they've been working on for fifteen."[19] The youth minister often feels he or she can never live up to parents' high expectations.

In addition to dealing with unrealistic expectations, the less experienced youth worker sometimes must cope with parents' suspicions and questions, often deserved, about his or her immature or unwise behavior. Unfortunately, the parent-youth minister relationship, which should be a powerful partnership of support and encouragement, often becomes a tension-filled scenario of distrust, backbiting and ill will.

The Problems of Youth. Puberty, that implosion of mischievous hormones, alters the human body with a violence second only to the trauma that takes place during the first two years of life. Although infants lack the self-awareness to reflect on their metamorphosis, adolescents are able to ponder their predicament with great anxiety.[20] Teenagers struggle, according to developmental psychologists, with ego, intellect and moral development using untried and immature coping and balancing mechanisms.[21] Inconsistency is one of the hallmarks of this age.

Contemporary youth culture of the 1980s tends to be egocentric at a crazed pace. Dr. Robert Ledge asserts:

The complexities and competitive pressures of modern life, combined with the symbols of success being available to practically everyone, have produced an anomic condition which manifests itself in self-oriented activity.

The specific content of the values which are indicative of this self orientation are traced to the countercultural movement of the Vietnam War generation. Use of drugs and permissive sexual standards, behaviors which characterize the present generation of youth represented the means by which the Vietnam War generation instilled solidarity against the war. Today drug use and sexual permissiveness symbolize the hedonistic, escapist self-orientation which dominates young people of our time.

Faced with the disillusioning events of the past decade, coupled with the introspective pressures generated by the anomie of affluence, today's youth have withdrawn from expressing concern about events occurring in society (which they feel helpless to control) to a concern about one's self. It appears that in the modern mass society, escapism and hedonism are symptomatic of the feeling that today people have nothing to believe in—no wars, no causes, no villains, no heroes. All that remains is the overwhelming cynicism of the times due to people's declining faith in the viability of the basic institutions of society.[22]

Keeping busy and having fun are kids' distractions from emptiness.[23] Because the youth minister's responsibility includes understanding and relating to the youth culture, youth programming tends to be fast-paced and action-oriented (and exhausting for the director). Constant activities, coupled with typical ministerial duties (counseling, administration, office hours, financial management, study, outreach, etc.,) produce tremendous pressure and stress for the youth minister.

When coupled with personal insecurities and immaturities, a youth minister's struggling to maintain self-esteem and a sense of mission in a low-rated ministry, striving to meet parents' high expectations for clarity and panting to keep pace with the narcissistic youth culture create the "drivenness" that plagues many youth workers. As Gordon MacDonald points out, "Driven people show the marks of stress," and Christ has "called those who were drawn to Him and avoided those who were driven and wanted to use him."[24]

How can the driven youth minister deal with these external and internal pressures and truly be useful to Christ Jesus? MacDonald answers: by ordering one's private world (spiritual formation). This can only be accomplished when one is "convinced that the inner world of the spiritual must govern the outer world of activity."[25]

Disciplines to Help Youth Ministers Flourish

Certainly, *all* the classical disciplines are crucial in helping the driven youth director order his or her private world. Yet the disciplines which seem most essential to a youth worker's spiritual formation can be categorized under solitude and accountability.

Solitude

As Henri Nouwen observes, "Without solitude it is virtually impossible to live a spiritual life. Solitude begins with a time and place for God, and Him alone."[26]

The youth minister must flee the sinking ship of ceaseless activity, selfish ambition and personal disarray. By seeking solitude of mind and heart, the youth worker can begin to be healed and cleansed from a false, sinful self; to discover his or her mission, giftedness and call; and to reorder his or her life and schedule. This desert experience is the fresh start most youth ministers need to escape the downward spiral so common in youth ministry.

Immaturity, egocentric motivation, disorganization and insecurity are root causes of the youth worker's drivenness. Nouwen notes that, "Solitude is the place of the great struggle and the great encounter—the struggle against the compulsions of the false self, and the encounter with the loving God who offers Himself as the Substance of the new self."[27]

Yet, fleeing to the solitude of the desert is only a means to the end of ordering one's life to allow time for daily inner attentiveness, study, worship, family and service. . . .[28]

To make following this discipline of solitude practical, a youth director should schedule a two-day prayer retreat alone with God. This retreat should include:

1. Rest and recreation—silence/settling;

2. Assessing one's past and present in light of God's clear will and word—meditation;

3. Dealing with sin, insecurities, damaged emotions—confession;

4. Receiving healing, forgiveness, cleansing, grace and giving thanks—celebration/worship;

5. Discovering God's will and call and his gifts and graces—study; and

6. Scheduling one's life in detail for one week—submission in creating quality time for God, family, mission, rest, etc.

In addition to this retreat, the youth worker should plan daily quiet times and weekly Sabbath times of solitude and silence with God in order to cultivate an attitude of abiding in God's presence. Richard Foster explains that, "If we possess inward solitude we will not fear being alone, for we know that we are not alone. Neither do we fear being with others, for they do not control us. In the midst of noise and confusion we are settled into a deep inner silence."[29]

Accountability

Intricately scheduled priority time with God, family and others is merely an empty good intention unless it is consistently practiced. Alas, the fly in the ointment! How can the youth minister follow a lofty schedule? The answer is accountability.

Webster defines "account" as "a statement or exposition of reasons, causes, grounds, or motives" and "to furnish a justifying analysis or explanation." Thus, the accountable youth minister will find outward motivations for the inward formation of an abiding relationship with Jesus.

Two practical ways to achieve accountability are journal keeping and growth partners.

Keeping a Record. Throughout history, many saints have kept spiritual journals. Such a journal helps a disciple examine motives, record God's dealings, analyze weaknesses and explain feelings and struggles. Gordon MacDonald suggests that one's journal ought to include, "An account of things that I accomplished in the preceding day, people I met, things I learned, feelings I experienced and impressions I believe God wanted me to have."[30] The spiritual journal helps the minister stay accountable to God by recording progress in spiritual formation.

Gathering Together. One of the first things we ought to do when we enter a parish is to find some fellow ministers (from other churches or organizations such as Young Life) we can meet with for fellowship and accountability.

The Scriptures exhort us to "consider how we may spur one another on toward love and good deeds. Let us not give up meeting together, as some are in the habit of doing, but let us encourage one another—and all the more as you see the Day approaching" (Hebrews 10:24-25).

This biblical command to hold one another accountable is not surprising in light of our pitiful state: ". . .sinful from the time my mother conceived me" (Psalm 51:5); "The heart is deceitful above all things and beyond cure" (Jeremiah 17:9); "All have sinned and fall short of the glory of God" (Romans 3:32). Left to ourselves, we are doomed to fail, even after conversion. The New Testament Christians widely depended on God and each other for growth, service and accountability (see Acts 2:41-47 and Romans 12:3-10). Likewise, the genius of the 18th-century Wesleyan revival was the Methodist Societies. These accountability groups required members to examine and account for their spiritual, moral and social lifestyles. This gave the Methodist revival world- and life-changing substance, not just emotion and fervor.

The youth minister who is serious about spiritual formation will do well to remember Solomon's words, "Two are better than one, because they have a good return for their work: If one falls down, his friend can help him up. But pity the man who falls and has no one to help him up! Also, if two lie down together, they will keep warm. But how can one keep warm alone? Though one may be overpowered, two can defend themselves. A cord of three strands is not quickly broken" (Ecclesiastes 4:9-12).

One Youth Worker's Experience

Early in my own spiritual pilgrimage, I tried to incorporate the discipline of solitude in my life. I planned to pray daily, spend time with God and use a journal and fellow Christians to help me be accountable in my walk with God. But as I tried to have a daily quiet time, real problems, areas of weakness and needs for radical change would often arise. As I studied God's Word, prayed and read the writings of the great spiritual fathers, I would feel the need to deal with those problems right then. But I knew that if I dealt with them immediately, it would take half the day!

This was the situation at least two or three times a week. I would often finish my quiet time in thirty minutes or an hour and a half or whatever it was, feeling a great sense of incompleteness—of frustration and despair over the need for more time to pay attention to these different areas. Sometimes my concerns were even burdens for other people, but knowing that I was expected to do ministry, my job, and was responsible to my family and other people, I could not spend adequate time grappling with these troubles in solitude.

On the other hand, sometimes I would find myself spending so much time tending the inward garden, trying to deal with every resistance within me and become impassioned to serve other people, that I would become reclusive. When this happened, I was not being faithful to my family or other people—I was just not getting the job of ministry done.

Eventually, I found a solution to this dilemma—rhythm. God created a world of seasons and rhythm—times of slowness and steadiness and times of suddenness and rapid growth. As I struggled with spiritual formation, I discovered that it was good for me to set up a daily devotional time with God. This generally lasts about thirty minutes to an hour. In this quiet time, I usually focus on just the basic disciplines—praise, adoration, singing hymns and spiritual songs, confession, studying the Scripture and intercession for other people. It is a time of spiritual union with Christ and opening my life to him and dedicating the day to him. I generally have this time in the morning.

But, I still often sense a need to spend more time alone with God because during that time of daily union with him, things surface that require a lot of prayer, self-examination and sometimes tremendous struggle. So I added what to me seemed a revolutionary new concept—the Sabbath. Actually, the idea is as old as the Old Testament, as old as the Torah itself. But I began to set aside my own Sabbath time.

Now, being a full-time minister, Sunday is the worst day to find time to spend apart with God. For me, the best time to do this is usually Saturday morning. My Sabbath, though it would be best to have it last all day long, generally runs from three to five hours. I find it must be at least three hours long to be effective, but after five hours it begins to seriously tax my schedule.

During my Sabbath time, I allow an extended period for the basic disciplines. Whereas the daily time allows opportunity for only ten or fifteen minutes of praise, worship and singing of hymns, during the Sabbath I might have the opportunity to praise God in a personal way for thirty minutes. Confession can be a time of extended prayer and soul searching as I confess my faith and the great creeds of the Scripture. The Anglican Prayer Book, the Scriptures and some of the writings of the early church fathers contain many great helps for confession and adoration.

During this Sabbath, there is time for extended thanksgiving and to prayer with depth and patience for other people. There is also time and opportunity for listening to God, studying his Word with attentiveness and memorizing Scripture.

Perhaps the most important aspect of my Sabbath is a time of evaluation. Using a journal, I ask three basic questions.

What Have I Done Right?

The first is, *What have I done well that is pleasing to God this week?* I list in detail the priorities I have used to set my schedule. I record what I have done in my relationship with God that is pleasing to him and that has been helpful with my family and my ministry. I evaluate my ministry, both administration and contact work, the time I spend with people and in preaching and teaching.

What Have I Done Wrong?

The second question I ask myself is, *What things have I done this week that are displeasing and unhelpful?* I evaluate the same categories as in the first question—God, family and ministry. I also assess self, including recreation and any project that I may be working on at the time.

What Am I Going to Do About It?

And the last question, which may be the most important, is, *What am I going to do about it?* At this point, I write a specific plan that will accentuate the good and try to counteract the bad.

Benefits of the Sabbath Time

Of the many benefits of the Sabbath time, for me two are the greatest. First, I tend to be the kind of person who—if I preach ten sermons a week, win two or three people to Christ, organize a wonderful program, meet with twenty young people one-on-one—will probably say if you ask me at the end of the week what I have done, "Oh, nothing." Like many people, I tend to feel like I am not doing enough; that I am not doing anything really significant for God. The Sabbath journal helps me see what I really *am* doing. It provides affirmation and relaxation. Also, the journal's record helps me recognize when I am honestly taking on much more than I can realistically expect to do well.

The Sabbath journal has also helped me break negative sin patterns in my life. Before I began having a weekly Sabbath, these sort of patterns could go on for months before I became aware of them. I would have a general feeling that I was making mistakes and that I was in sin, but I wouldn't really define what was going on. Sometimes it would be several months before I would do anything concrete to overcome these problems or sins. But my Sabbath journaling gives me time each week to evaluate those sinful patterns, to accentuate good patterns and to make plans with God to overcome negative trends.

Take a Monthly Festival

Often, however, these daily and weekly times become monotonous or do not provide enough time for me to really relax and be quiet in my spirit so that I can receive direction, correction or affirmation from God. Therefore, I began celebrating a monthly festival. I set aside one day a month—eight to ten hours. Usually I go to the sanctuary of our church or to the local seminary or college chapel and spend a day before God, rather than just thirty minutes or an hour and a half. I read the Psalms and works of adoration to praise God and focus on his greatness and who he is. Also, I allow plenty of time for confession and earnestly seeking God's face for forgiveness and for a spirit of steadfastness and repentance. Again I use the Scripture and spiritual helps. This monthly festival also includes time for thanksgiving and for longer intercessory prayer. If I feel the need to pray for many people—for families and concerns in my ministry—this is an opportunity to do so. I study portions of the Scriptures, the Torah, the historical books, the prophets and the wisdom literature, the Gospels and the Epistles. These help me grasp the big picture of what God wants to say. Listen to God, relax, unwind—as the Psalm says, "Be still, and know that I am God. . ." (Psalm 46:10).

During this monthly festival, I use the same method of journaling, except that I evaluate the month instead of the week. I ask myself what I have done this month that has been pleasing to God, what I have done that is counterproductive to the kingdom and what I am going to do about it.

I also use this monthly time as an opportunity to evaluate my ministry, both the program and the contact work, and to make plans for the coming month. I review what has been done in light of our overall goals and plans for that ministry period.

Enjoy a Jubilee

Lastly, twice a year I observe what I call the time of Jubilee. This idea comes from Scripture and was a tradition of the early Israelites. I schedule my Jubilees in early January and late August. This personal retreat lasts three days.

Usually I spend the first day just slowing down. Because my usual pace is so hectic, it takes me a day just to get still inside. Then I begin to spend extended times in praise and adoration, confession, thanksgiving, intercessory prayer and study (reading devotional material of various sorts, both contemporary writing as well as works by the spiritual masters of the early church).

Again, I keep a journal, this time focusing on the last six months. I go into great detail in the journal, describing ways I have grown in my relationship with God and my family, in the ministry and in my own personal life.

Next, I formulate a schedule for the next six months, building on the good and learning from the bad what to do differently. In this schedule, I also try to incorporate the insights gained from my Jubilee time with God. This schedule covers all aspects of my life and ministry; I use it as my personal formation schedule, family schedule, and ministry schedule. Here I set the goals and the themes of my ministry for the next six months. I try to plan, at least initially, future youth activities, which I later present to our parents and our ministry team for perfecting through their input.

Why You Need Times of Spiritual Renewal

I've discovered that one of the benefits of this rhythm of spiritual discipline is that when I spend extended time with God on a daily, weekly, monthly and yearly basis, I derive my sense of self-esteem from God's love for me, his affirmation and his grace instead of from my performance or what others do or do not affirm about me and my ministry.

Another benefit is that my inner world becomes ordered, as Gordon MacDonald describes it. My inward perspective about God and others becomes clearer. My relationship with God flourishes—my love for God is impassioned by these times. Devoting this time to spiritual formation also helps me become more honest about myself—I have a more realistic self-image and self-view. I realize I am not the Messiah, I can just do so much, and I can only do that through the grace of God. I become aware of my deep and genuine sin and weakness and that I need help from God and others if I am to have any hope of an effective life or ministry.

These rhythms of discipline also increase the balance in my life. I realize God's love and his blessing in every dimension—emotionally, recreationally, academically, spiritually and socially. Indeed, God has made us multi-faceted. We need to pay attention to each facet of our created being so that we can live that abundant life for which Jesus died.

Another benefit of times of spiritual discipline is a greater sensitivity to sin. Not only am I more aware of sin in my life but, more importantly, of victory. These quiet times are an opportunity to gain the perspective, spiritual power and biblical insight needed to deal with and gain victory over sin.

These spiritual rhythms also give a direction or vision for ministry. My ministry is born out of prayer on a daily, weekly, monthly and yearly basis as I pray methodically for the people over whom I have charge. These people are my sheep, if you will, for whom God has made me the shepherd. As I pray for them, I gain compassion and a sense of direction in ministry. The insight gained from these quiet times is based on Scripture and prayer, which are better foundations for our program than the whim of the moment, the wishes of moms and dads or the current popular trend in youth ministry. (We would hope we use all of those things, too, to enhance programs, but the wellspring of direction in ministry should come from our prayer, praise and spiritual formation time.)

Finally, for me the most significant benefit has been that the more time I spend with God and his Word, the more I find myself genuinely in love with God, other people, my family and myself in a wholesome way. And that, as I understand the Scriptures, is the heart of the matter. It is the principle in which all the law and the prophets find their completion (see Matthew 22:37-40). So, having witnessed more love being born in my life through these spiritual disciplines, I am convinced that they are something we youth ministers and youth workers can never view as a nice option. Spiritual formation is an all-encompassing necessity. We must focus, first and foremost, on building our relationship with God when we enter ministry.

Spiritual formation truly is the youth minister's taproot. Daily practice of the disciplines, in order to abide in Jesus, is the key to healthy, loving and effective living and ministry. Nurturing a personal, vital relationship with God must remain our first priority. Jesus commands us, "Seek first his kingdom and his righteousness, and all these things will be given to you as well" (Matthew 6:33).

A Good Youth Ministry Home

Avoiding the Manic Ministry Personality

By Hule Goddard

Family breakdown seems to be a tragic hallmark of contemporary evangelical ministry. Today, when ministers' marriages and families fall apart, it has become the butt of jokes. Of course, ministers' children have long been stereotyped as hellions. You know the old cliché—look out for the preacher's kid! Perhaps because we ministers have so often failed to have our families be what God wants them to be, our children are expected to be wild and unruly. But we realize how far that is from God's intention as we read the Scriptures describing his requirements for ministers, overseers and deacons and their families!

Many of our problems as youth ministers stem from young people's problems at home. Our struggles often involve young people who haven't developed properly because of some family breakdown. We see how these young people become grossly insecure, warped and very difficult to work with. So we youth workers, more than other people, should be dedicated to spending quality time with our families and doing whatever it takes to raise children who have a sense of security and stability in the love and grace of God. Unfortunately, however, that doesn't seem to be the case. Often, especially in our evangelical community, we see occurs in the most successful youth ministers. In fact, it seems the more successful they are, the more this manic ministry personality tends to emerge and to undermine their effectiveness as spouses and parents.

How the Youth Minister's Family Can Suffer—One Man's Story

Let me explain what I mean by the manic ministry personality by describing my own unfortunate early experiences in the ministry. When I was about nineteen or twenty years old, I began my youth ministry. My supervisors and I had ignored the apostle Paul's suggestion in 1 Timothy 3:6 that an overseer, one who is in charge of the lives of others, should not be a recent convert. Let that person be one who has been tried, let him be tested, let him have an opportunity to learn and mature. *Then,* if he proves to be faithful, appoint him as an overseer.

Well, unfortunately, I wasn't tried and hadn't matured. I still had much to learn about my own self-identity and self-esteem. I still hadn't worked through a healthy expression of my own sexuality. In so many facets of my life I wasn't ready to lead other people, especially adolescents with the same sort of struggles.

The greatest drawback to my immaturity was that I derived my self-esteem and self-concept from the praise and approval of those for whom I did ministry. When a person begins ministry, the older women in the church, parents and even the young people begin to affirm that person. That approval became my bread and meat. When I did well and was praised, I believed I was worthy. But when I was not praised, I felt I was not worthy, and my opinion of myself was very low. So in addition to all the other problems of a typical late adolescent, I had made the mistake of using ministry as the bedrock of my self-esteem. Thus, my personality was inseparable from my ministry. Through the years, this gave me many problems and led to my developing the manic ministry personality.

After I was married, I continued to strive to excel in ministry because I felt that was my source of goodness and worth. I made a fatal mistake in family life by misinterpreting the passage in which Jesus says, "Anyone who loves his father or mother more than me is not worthy of me; anyone who loves his son or daughter more than me is not worthy of me; and anyone who does not take his cross and follow me is not worthy of me," to mean that we must deny ourselves and our families. When any conflict arose between ministry to other people's needs and my own needs as a husband, or my wife's needs, I would deny us, even though I often longed with all my heart to be with my new bride whom I loved so much. Even when we had plans, if a ministry situation arose, I would quickly call my wife and cancel our plans.

For a while, it was all right, but eventually this behavior became a habit. Our family life was often undermined and diminished by the great demands of ministry. Of course, the reason these demands were so great in our early days of ministry and marriage was because I equated every need with God's will. I saw every need in my church, youth group or community that had anything to do with teenagers as the call of God for me.

This created enough of a burden when we served in a small county seat town in Mississippi, but when we moved to inner-city Dallas, that load became unbearable. My days were never, ever long enough for me to even scratch the surface of what I wanted to do. As I tried to reach everyone who had a need, I found myself in a frenzied state. The more I did, the more people praised me and the more I wanted to do in ministry. The more people affirmed me, the better I felt. My self-image became so intertwined with what I did that I continued to neglect my relationship with my wife and, by that time, our little girl.

This went on for a number of years until one Fourth of July when my wife finally shared with me her brokenness. She told me how the years of trying to be faithful to God, to me and to our call to ministry had left her so often without a husband's care. We frequently had no time together at all, much less the quality time needed to build family relationships. Because I often worked twelve to sixteen hours a day, or was gone for weeks at a time and weekends, there just wasn't time for family. As she shared her sorrow with me, I realized that I was wrong and I had to do something. I had said, since my early days of faith, that one's priorities ought to be God first, family second and ministry or job third. But I had never lived up to that a day in my life!

From that time on, we set aside a family time one day every week. But rather than adjust my priorities and elevate my family to its proper place, I simply pushed my ministry into high gear. Since I now had less time to do what I had been doing, I added more pressure to my manic ministry personality. By the time our family day came, I would be so exhausted from having sprinted all the harder to make time for this twenty-four-hour period, that I was only there physically. I was a zombie! As our family met together, I would have little to say and no feelings to express. The more I got caught up in this vicious circle, the less I was able, emotionally and spiritually, to love God or my family. I was burned out, numb and desperate inside, but somehow didn't understand any other way of doing ministry.

Finally, my manic ministry personality began to wind down when we moved from Dallas to Wilmore, Kentucky, a small community whose slower pace allowed more time for family and spiritual formation. However, the manic ministry personality can put in a fourteen-hour day wherever it lives.

After we moved to Wilmore, my wife and I decided to take a vacation together for the first time since the birth of our oldest child. We would leave Sarah Jo with her grandmothers and go to Wyoming on a backpacking trip. During this vacation, I planned to ascend Bomber peak to celebrate my thirtieth birthday.

When we were out in the wilderness, the mosquitoes were horrendous and Loretta had to spend much of her time in the tent. We decided that since we had a lot of time on our hands we would use some of it to evaluate our lives, our marriage and our spiritual conditions. To do so, I hiked up to one of the most majestic spots in all the world. All around me were beautiful mountain peaks. I was above the treeline, and the meadows were filled with mountain flowers of astounding beauty. It was as though I were in the narthex of heaven itself. There I began to evaluate my thirty years and especially the last ten years of my ministry.

At first I felt really affirmed. I came up with a straw figure of twenty-five or thirty thousand young people whose lives I had touched in some way. As I enumerated my accomplishments, I sat higher and higher on those rocks. But then I settled into a deeper introspection, and I began to see a problem. I had to ask myself why I had done these things. Why had I pushed myself so hard and worked such long days? As the answer came, I slipped off that rock down onto my knees. Examining my ministry, I saw that much of what I had accomplished had been done for personal glory and honor. I had done many right things for the wrong reasons—to bolster my self-concept rather than purely out of love for God. Some of my motives were pure, but too much of my ministry had been done for self-centered purposes.

Then as I examined my performance as a husband and father, I saw how desperately lacking I was. I saw that even if I won every teenager in the Western world to Christ I would still be a failure if my own wife and daughters lived lives of emptiness and abandonment because I had ignored my first responsibility. As I reflected on what would really matter when I was seventy years old and looking back on my life, I decided that the most important thing would not be those thousands of young people I had reached, but would be my relationship with God and with Loretta and Sarah Jo (and since then with Julianne).

Coming back from the mountains, I was somehow different inside. I began to look to God and to study the Scriptures to learn his plan for family in the life of the Christian minister.

What the Bible Teaches About the Role of the Minister's Family

The first thing that struck me in the 1 Timothy 3 passage was the requirement that an overseer, a person qualified to be a minister, must be a person who manages his own family well and whose children obey him with proper respect. If anyone does not know how to manage his own family, how can he take care of God's church? (See 1 Timothy 3:4-5). What a powerful thing the Scriptures say to us as ministers! Before we involve ourselves in leadership roles in the church, God requires us to be competent overseers at home. To be effective pastors, we have to learn and practice ministry at home first.

When I studied the Scriptures as a whole, I found that the Bible is a book about families. In the very beginning, even before the creation of the world, a family existed which, as the apostle Paul says in Ephesians 3:15, every "family in heaven and on earth derives its name." The family is part of God's character. God created the first human family. He worked with families throughout the Scriptures. God has interacted with families from Genesis to Revelation. We find that family, God, life and church (the people of God) are inseparable. In the Bible, God's primary avenue for reaching us as persons and helping us mature is through the family.

In Deuteronomy 4:9, parents are commanded to teach their children and their children's children the ways and the mighty acts of God. In Deuteronomy 6:7-9, one of the most powerful and oft-quoted passages of the Old Testament, God commands the people of Israel to love the Lord their God with all their hearts and souls and to impress his commands on their children: "Talk about them when you sit at home and when you walk along the road, when you lie down and when you get up." God is saying every aspect of our lives at home should provide training in his ways. The apostle Paul echoes this concept in Ephesians 6:4: "Fathers, do not exasperate your children; instead, bring them up in the training and instruction of the Lord." God requires us as Christians and ministers to be his first line of teaching and ministry to our children. The family should be the most basic unit in the body of Christ.

God's desires for the family are also vividly revealed in his Son. Jesus, Hebrews says, is the exact representation of God to us, and Jesus was born in a family. Jesus grew up in the context of a strong Jewish home. His mother and father obeyed God's commands and gave the proper sacrifices for him. Luke 2:40 tells us that Jesus developed in favor with God and man as he grew in stature and wisdom.

The Bible also tells us that Jesus stayed at home until he was thirty years old. That has always astonished me. Where do we see more graphically God's high regard for the family than in that fact that Jesus, God with skin on, stayed at home for thirty years? During that thirty years people were dying and going to hell. People were suffering, wounded, leprous, deceived, mentally demented and languishing in need. Yet God, who had all the power in heaven and earth, stayed at home and attended his family. Evidently, Joseph had passed away and Jesus needed to stay at home and care for his mother and younger brothers. (We don't *know* that Joseph passed away, but for whatever reason, Jesus stayed.) God in human flesh set the example that family is our first priority, and ministry to other people must come in its proper time and place.

During Jesus' public ministry, his family probably misunderstood him and at times thought he had lost his mind and become unstable. They apparently even came to get him at one point (see Matthew 12:46-47). Still, as he hung on the cross amid amazing agony and pain, one of his last thoughts was of his mother. As he saw her standing there, he entrusted her into the care of his good friend John (see John 19:25-27).

Jesus' family life didn't end with the cross and the resurrection. Mary and Jesus' brothers were present in the upper room (see Acts 1:14). Jesus' physical family was also there when the Holy Spirit was poured out and the church was born. In fact, one of Jesus' brothers, James, was a pillar of, and maybe the primary leader of, the early church, especially the Jewish church. He was the one who spoke up in Acts 15:13-19 and gave the quarreling Jerusalem Council the scriptural view needed to end the dissention between the Gentile and Jewish Christians. So we find that the family was central in Jesus' life and even seemed to have priority over ministry.

But perhaps the clearest word in Scripture about our responsibility to our families is found in 1 Timothy 5:8: "If anyone does not provide for his relatives, and especially for his immediate family, he has denied the faith and is worse than an unbeliever." No other sin, except for blasphemy against the Holy Spirit, is as strongly condemned as neglecting family. The apostle Paul is saying that if we don't provide for our families, we have denied everything that is Christlike and everything that has to do with loving God and genuinely loving others. We may profess with our mouths that we love God and are followers of Christ, but our lives contradict that if we don't care for those who live in our household, who are our first responsibility after God. Paul says such a person is worse than an unbeliever. Even most unbelievers, the self-centered persons who ignore God, take care of their own families. Therefore, a person who does not nurture his or her own family does worse than most people who have no faith at all.

In that same chapter, verse 4, Paul says people should practice their religion by providing for their own families and that this is pleasing to God. So the Scriptures clearly teach that our responsibility to others starts with the family. Only our relationship with God should come before our care for our families.

Unique Strains on the Youth Minister's Family

The youth worker's family life faces numerous unique stresses and conflicts. These conflicts are rooted in theology, youth culture and ministry demands. Our evangelical background helps us in youth ministry see the tremendous need around us. We know that the world is lost without Jesus and that our era of history could very likely be the last days. This tends to spur us to get busy, and therefore our priorities sometimes get muddled.

We also face the common tendency of the helping professions to diminish and squeeze out family life. Doctors, ministers, emergency technicians and others who help the public in desperate times of need do not have eight-to-five jobs. As crises and emergencies arise, those in the helping professions must respond, which greatly taxes their family lives.

In youth ministry, we not only have those pressures to deal with, but also some unique strains on family life. For example, the times that young people are available, after school and early evenings, are often traditional family times. Weekends are also prime times for youth programs and relational ministry activities. Young people also tend to be free and willing to involve themselves in youth activities during the holidays. The summer, which is usually a time for family vacations and outdoor activities, is another time when youth ministry programs are in high gear. These activities involve us, exhaust us and leave us with little time and motivation to be with our families.

Another distraction from the youth minister's family life is the youth culture. The pace, the attitude and the rhythm of the youth culture tend not to be family oriented. Young people, as mentioned in earlier chapters, are trying to establish themselves as independent individuals. They are not living apart from their families, but they usually have a need to step away from the family. The youth culture is a self culture that thrives on being with peers and participating in activities away from the family. We as youth ministers must minister to young people in their intense and fast-moving culture. Because the youth culture just does not normally lend itself to family life, we often face a conflict when we try to spend quality time in family activities.

Finally, If you are involved in ministry of any kind, and especially relational ministry, you often deal with people in pain and various crises. This drains you, sapping your emotional energy, so that when you get home all you want to do is crash. You have little intensity, love or energy left for your spouse and children. Thus the typical youth minister is torn between trying to be an effective family member and meeting the demands of ministry. God's call to give ourselves fully and energetically to our families often seems to compete with his call to give ourselves fully and energetically to the young people to whom we minister.

Some Practical Solutions

Here are some suggestions to help you be God's man or woman of faith as well as heed his command to minister to your own family.

The Family Retreat. The first thing to remember is

Peter's message in Acts 2:37 to the people present at Pentecost who asked, "Brothers, what shall we do?" Peter replied, "repent." That seems like a simplistic answer, but it is the most powerful thing we can do. Somehow, we have got to stop walking in the direction of misplaced priorities, overcommitment and manic ministry. We must repent.

The best way I know to do this is to take a personal or a family retreat. Take a sabbatical, if you need to, from your ministry responsibilities. Evaluate your life, ask the hard questions and look at the ministry you are doing. Examine your family life and the kind of ministry you have there, and scrutinize your relationship with God. If necessary, reorder the priorities in your life. Decide to make God the real number one priority and make your family your first human responsibility, the first people to whom you minister.

After repenting we need to commit ourselves to a new way of living. Now, I am not proposing a cathartic emotional upheaval. I am not even proposing turning over a new leaf. Rather, I am talking about radical repentance that changes the very way we live—our attitudes, perspectives and activities.

Make a New Schedule. After taking the family retreat, reschedule your life as much as necessary to change it. Schedule time every day for spiritual formation. (See chapter nine for more on this subject.) Next, include in that schedule daily time to be with your family. Touch base with your mate and your children, whether during the dinner meal, at breakfast or before bedtime. Decide what will work for you and your family. I also suggest that you reserve a weekly family day. During this day, be sure to include family devotions so that God's nurture will be a family matter as well as a personal one.

When devising your schedule, look ahead and plan family weekend activities and vacations. Almost every older man or woman who reminisces about the things they are glad they did and the things that they regret will say, "I wish I had taken more family vacations." Many of our fondest memories are of our family vacation times, so I plead with you to schedule a vacation of at least a week or longer every year. Go somewhere; borrow the money if you have to. What better investment can you make than in your family life? (Certainly, saving and including vacation expenses in your budget are better ways to prepare, but if you have to, borrow the money.) Is your family really your number one priority after God? If it is, you will come up with the money, and you will make the time.

Get Some Rhythm. I also encourage you to gain a sense of rhythm and pace in your life. Our lives must proceed at a tempo that leaves us energy at the end of the day to give to our families. We must also pace our lives so that we can still be effective in ministry when we are forty or fifty years old. The young people we serve live as though there is no tomorrow. They have energy to spare. But that's not true for us adults who minister to them, so we must pace ourselves. (This is difficult because we must walk at our pace as we minister to young people who are walking at their more frenzied pace.)

We need a sense of rhythm in our lives. Nature ought to tell us this. We in the Western world try to make our bodies, our minds, our emotions, our families, our ministries and our relationships with God run like the machines that we produce and almost worship. But this is not characteristic of human beings or any living things in nature. Our world is a cyclical world. Seasons come and go, our bodies grow and wither, our ability to concentrate and work peaks and falls. We are not machines that work at the same speed every day, and we have to schedule ourselves in light of this truth. Incorporate into the rhythms of your life seasons of intense work and ministry *and* seasons in which your major focus is your family.

Every person's schedule will be different. For example, I have been in Wilmore long enough to know the seasons of our ministry. We have a very intense ministry during the fall, so I prepare for that by planning family weekends to compensate. I also know that the holiday season here brings a lull in ministry duties, and I can use that time to build family relationships with my wife, daughters and extended family. In Wilmore the pace is also slower in the summertime, so I dedicate the month of July to family. That is not to say that I do not go to work, but the major focus of my planning and energy for that month is on family. The rhythms of ministry in your situation may be very different. However, the efforts we make to plan seasons for family life bring richness, power and depth to our family relationships.

Don't Try to Do It All. Finally, and this is probably the most important suggestion, realize that you cannot do it all. You are not the Messiah. The person who *is* the Messiah ought to be an example to us. Jesus had it all when he lived on earth—the power to heal, to save and to transform the world forever. Yet, in the Bible we never read about Jesus scurrying from need to need, frantically, neurotically trying to heal every sickness that he saw in the world. Instead, we find that Jesus, with great purpose, ministered to the crowds as time and availability gave him the opportunity. He trained the seventy and spent most of his time discipling the twelve. Finally, he intensely prepared the three (Peter, James and John) for leadership. And yet Jesus seemed to get up every morning and walk with God through that day. He had a plan in what he was doing.

We do not have a fingernail's worth of Jesus' power to minister. Comparing us to Jesus, who was God incarnated, is like comparing a grain of sand to the beach. Yet, we try to do it all. We rush about trying to meet every need.

How can we stop this frenzied behavior? First, we must daily and weekly discern, as best we can, what is God's will. Then we should give ourselves to doing that. As we plan our schedules, we must allow time for God first, family second and then our ministry. God will show us the things that we need to do. I believe he will also reveal to us things that we are doing that are not worthy of our time.

Simplicity

Simplicity is a discipline that every Christian, especially the youth minister, needs to practice. Simplicity is one of the oldest Christian disciplines. It was championed by St. Francis of Assisi, a rich merchant's son who forsook the distractions of this world so that he could simply love God and love others. We twentieth-century Christians also need to simplify. We need to focus on activities, attitudes and commitments that enhance our love for God, our love for our families and our love for other people. We ought to delete or diminish whatever does not enhance our ability to love. Practicing the discipline of simplicity will go a long way toward limiting our over-commitment. Our frenzied pace and our culture's preoccupation with unnecessary possessions and responsibilities are great distractions to our being effective ministers.

Flexibility and Creativity

We must also be flexible and creative. My wife shares, in the following article, some of her struggles as a youth minister's wife. She offers some good advice about being flexible and creative.

Loretta Goddard Reflects Upon Being the Wife of a Youth Minister

As the wife of a youth minister, I've been asked to write some kind of article on life as "his wife." Since I have no experience being the husband of a youth minister, I won't address this issue, though I know it exists.

I wish I had some idea of where to begin. Though I've been married to a youth minister for more than ten years, I haven't found any miraculous recipe for being successful at it. Books and magazines about life as a pastor's wife have been helpful, but their insights don't always apply to our situation, and many important youth ministry scenarios remain unexplored.

One of the biggest adjustments I've had to make is to erase all of my preconceived ideas about an "8 to 5" time frame and accept that our lifestyle would run on a "5:30 a.m. - 12:00 noon," then "3:00 p.m. to 6:00 p.m. or 9:30 p.m. or . . .?" schedule. This has taken years. If I hadn't abandoned my preconceived expectations, our daily lives would be in constant turmoil, and the success of Hule's ministry would be very limited. (I know this because I can still remember the turmoil we experienced before I made this adjustment.)

This doesn't mean I've given up the ideas of romance, friendship or family time. It just means that Hule and I have arranged our schedule around prime youth times so that we spend time together when the youth aren't available. I get to see Hule for long lunches most days during the school year. Our children and I go along on as many youth activities as we can. Also, Hule makes dates with me on Friday nights when most of the kids are at the movies or out on dates of their own. He takes our two daughters on "prowls" with him to watch ball and band practices—they love it because they get extra attention while their daddy is practicing relational ministry.

Now, the summer months are another story. We have to schedule our vacations and family times before any youth events are planned and stick to our guns. This, for us, has been a key to sanity in the summer.

After serving in three churches I know that young people's schedules vary, and the timetable I've just described may not apply to your situation. The point is that the youth minister's wife should accept that she will usually live an unconventional, though, I would hope, creative and exciting, lifestyle.

I could give a million and one "tips" to the wife of a youth minister, but since this is Hule and Jorge's book, not mine, these ten will suffice:

1. Shedule, Schedule, Schedule

About five years into this unpredictable lifestyle, I began to feel out of control. It seemed that the youth were dictating our schedule. To recapture the feeling of control, we established the habit of making a schedule of monthly, weekly, daily and hourly happenings. We schedule anything from a weekend getaway once a month to a weekly family day to daily quiet time to exact times for Hule to come home each day or get home from Bible study. This schedule helps me remember what to expect and helps us evaluate more objectively whether we're becoming overcommitted. We usually adjust our weekly schedule a few times a year as programs change.

2. Respect your husband and his work

Besides being a command from God (Ephesians

5:33), *respecting your husband will go a long way towards assuring the success of his ministry. If his wife believes in him and tells him so, he's sure to strive for excellence. Youth ministry isn't one of the top ten most respected occupations. Many people, including those in your church, think your spouse might not have been good enough to be a "real" minister, so he is pastoring youth. Your respect for the importance of his work can help dispel the notion that youth ministry is just a stepping-stone to bigger and better things.*

3. Pray with, and for, your husband and the youth

Praying for your husband is a great way to be involved in his ministry. When Tina finally becomes a Christian after months of your prayers together, you can better share in the excitement of her conversion. When you've prayed for Ralph during his weekly counseling sessions with your husband, you feel a part of the teenager's final victory over drugs. And when you're praying for your husband, who is rappeling down a 150-foot rock with twenty teenagers, you're not quite so apprehensive.

4. Attend youth meetings and activities whenever possible

This increases your respect for your husband and his ministry. It also gives the youth a chance to see Christian marriage and family life in action. And because you have a chance to hear the announcements, you will know what to tell Bobby when he calls at 6:05 a.m. to ask whether the sixth graders can go to the amusement park next week!

5. Don't let your husband "run out of fun" with the youth

Hule doesn't like amusement parks any more, and at the end of a summer full of wilderness trips, he's not even so keen on a family campout. These are the pitfalls of too much "icing on the cake." When we're smart, we think ahead and let the other counselors lead some of these "fun" trips so our vacation to Disney World and state park camping areas doesn't seem like just another stress camp to Hule.

6. Take the phone off the hook if you need to

An answering maching, as cold as it may seem, can help to screen calls when you're feeling overwhelmed. (I've been tempted to make a new recording before each major trip listing all of the little details that kids miss when they're talking during youth meeting announcements.) Let the youth know who your backup is for real crises, and you won't feel so guilty about not being available twenty-four hours a day, seven days a week, 365 days a year.

7. Minister where your gifts are

I am not a gifted teacher. I need about one month of preparation to teach a one-hour Bible study. I read five books on the subject and have ten times more information than I need by the time I finally jitter through the session. On the other hand, I'm a great organizer. I can plan menus and shop for one hundred youth and make zillions of lists for Hule at youth events and on trips. I feel very comfortable doing what I do best and enjoying it rather than forcing myself to be someone I'm not. This way I am truly a "suitable helper" (Genesis 2:20b).

8. Talk with your husband about your feelings of jealousy and resentment

At times I have felt like I was competing with the ministry for Hule's attention and time. I felt this way especially when we were first married. I was only eighteen years old, had moved far away from my family and friends and was the same age as some of the girls in the youth group. Sometimes I felt pretty insecure when Hule spent time with these other girls my age. However, I was too ashamed to admit my feelings. When I finally did, a few years later, it was such a release. Hule became much more sensitive to me and my need to be established as his "number one lady."

9. Help your husband slow down and see the sunshine

This is not a problem for some people, but many youth ministers seem to become overcommitted. Encouraging your husband to take a day off to pursue his own hobbies or to take a mini-vacation to fulfill some dreams he's suppressed can help to unpeel the blinders around his eyes that come from intense overcommitment.

10. Praise God for this special role!

Being the wife of a youth minister doesn't have to be a curse. It can be a blessing. Life for you and your family will be much easier if you focus on the advantages rather than the disadvantages of this special calling. "Finally, [sisters], whatever is true, whatever is noble, whatever is right, whatever is pure, whatever is lovely, whatever is admirable—if anything is excellent or praiseworthy—think about such things" (Phillippians 4:8).

Since the youth culture and the times youth are available tend to conflict with traditional family times, we youth ministers must create a non-traditional family life and schedule. I find that here in Wilmore my ministry peaks before school, right after school and on weekends, so I try to create my family time at other times. Most days I spend two or three hours at home in the middle of the day to compensate for the evenings I am gone. A lot of my neighbors and church members do not really understand this, but I have to take that risk because our daily family time together at lunch is of major importance.

I must also be flexible in planning dates with my wife and weekend family retreats. I schedule these events first, putting them on the calendar before I plan any youth group events. If Loretta and I do not sit down and plan our family events first, ministry activities always squeeze out the family times.

Another creative solution that works in Wilmore (mentioned in earlier chapters) is meeting with youth at breakfast and early in the morning. I have breakfast almost every morning with youth or a group of youth, and our young people amazingly respond and look forward to this. Breakfast meetings may not be feasible in other communities, but you can find other untraditional ministry times that do not particularly tax your family times.

Finally, we must remind ourselves that whatever is important to God is important to youth ministry. If God wants family to be our first priority after our relationship with him, then it is the right thing to do for youth ministry. We draw the encouragement, inspiration and experience we need to be effective youth ministers from our families. If we are not at peace at home, we cannot have the perspective and the skills we need to be high quality youth ministers.

It is very effective, in this day of fragmented families, to model before young people a healthy family life. I try to model a husband who loves his wife deeply and passionately and a dad who loves his kids unconditionally while holding them to a pattern of discipline that will keep them from self-destructive activities.

We in youth ministry should heed what the apostle Paul told Timothy long ago. Let us first learn to practice our faith at home, and then we will be equipped and qualified to be effective overseers and workers with youth. If we follow God's plan, we will not have to abandon our family or produce havoc in our own children to be used of God to raise up a new generation of young people who will change our world.

The Player-Coach Approach

By Jorge Acevedo

In 1984, the Cincinnati Reds announced that Pete Rose, a member of the "Big Red Machine" baseball team of the 1970s, was returning to the team as a player-coach. As coach, he would ultimately be responsible for the Reds' success, yet like the rest of the team, he too would stand in the batter's box. Pete had the delicate task of guiding and participating. If they lost, he was responsible as both a player and as the coach.

I think this is the model for those of us who work with young people, whether as a volunteer or a part-time or full-time youth minister. Like Pete, we provide direction and leadership for the program, but we are only one among many necessary team members. In this chapter, we'll examine team ministry. We will study the biblical imperative to share our ministry. And, in our attempt to be practical, we will look at some ways of recruiting, training and caring for ministry team members.

Team Ministry and the Bible

I Am Not a Rock. I Am Not an Island!

Many folks always want to do any task on their own. This kind of person thinks, "I can do it better myself, so I won't ask anybody else to help." In America, where our attitude is often "pull yourself up by your own bootstraps," we have difficulty seeing the need to share any task. The sad thing is that this is also the attitude of many church leaders toward ministry.

From a biblical perspective, however, the need for a shared ministry is affirmed as both right and practical. For example, the Old Testament tells how the recently freed Hebrews were complaining to the rugged, aging Moses (see Numbers 11:1-17). They pined for the food they had in Egypt: fish, cucumbers, melons, leeks, onions and garlic (imagine their breath!). They were tired of eating manna.

Moses was angry at the people, but he was also mad at God. "Why have you brought this trouble on your servant?" he asked the Lord. ". . . Did I conceive all these people? Did I give them birth? Why do you tell me to carry them in my arms, as a nurse carries an infant, to the land you promised on oath to their forefathers? Where can I get meat for all these people? They keep wailing to me, 'Give us meat to eat!'" And then Moses put the icing on the cake when he said, "I cannot carry all these people by myself; the burden is too heavy for me. If this is how you are going to treat me, put me to death right now—if I have found favor in your eyes—and do not let me face my own ruin" (11:11-15). The sheer number of people and their problems had overwhelmed Moses. Their grumbling had become too much for one person to endure.

God responded to Moses by saying, "Bring me seventy of Israel's elders who are known to you as leaders . . . to the Tent of Meeting, that they may stand there with you. I will come down and speak with you there, and I will take of the Spirit that is on you and put the Spirit on them. They will help you carry the burden of the people so that you will not have to carry it alone" (11:16-17). God appointed persons from the people of Israel to be burden bearers with Moses. What a dynamic illustration of team ministry! Notice that the Spirit who was in Moses was also placed in the ministers. The vision that had belonged only to Moses was now shared with his new partners in ministry.

It is essential that those of us who work with youth realize that we cannot do it all. We are not rocks or islands. The burden of ministry to even ten youth is too much for one youth worker to bear. We must share our ministry.

The Neck Bone's Connected to the . . .

Another powerful biblical passage describing team ministry is 1 Corinthians 12:12-31. Paul uses the human body as an analogy to explain the nature of the Church. The Church of Jesus Christ is like a body with its many parts. Each part is necessary. Like the various parts of the body, we all have different spiritual gifts to help the Church accomplish its ministry.

In 12:18, Paul says, "God has arranged the parts in the body, every one of them, just as he wanted them to be." God designed the Church to be whole and complete. We in youth ministry need to realize that many people are called by God to work with youth. There may be young couples, college students, divorced or retired persons whom God is calling to work with youth in your church. As the youth leader, you need to help them fulfill this calling. More than once someone has told me, "I thought I would be the last person called to do youth work. But God has called me to work with teenagers and has given me the ability and patience to do it!" Help the body of Christ be complete. Seek out those led by God to be on the youth ministry team in your church.

Jesus and the Team

Jesus gave us perhaps the ultimate example of a shared ministry. More than one scholar has noted that Jesus equipped the twelve to do ministry during the three and a half years of his own earthly ministry. Jesus shared his ministry with the disciples despite all of their shortcomings. By sharing the ministry, Jesus maximized his investment of time and energy because the disciples made possible even further-reaching ministry.

When we nurture those called of God to work with youth, we maximize our investment too! When I served at Trinity Hill, we had about one hundred active youth. No way could I even begin to get to know all of them. So we built a ministry team of ten to fifteen people, each of whom could get to know a few youth. In this way, we multiplied our effectiveness and were able to have an impact on more young people.

Team Ministry: The Practical Side

Have I Got a Job for You!—Recruiting a Ministry Team

Military recruiting posters used to say, "Uncle Sam wants you!" This is the way many of us approach recruiting people to work with our youth groups. We know we need some help with the youth, so we announce at church or in the newsletter, "We need help with the youth ministry. Can you help?" The problem with this method is that it is indiscriminate. It communicates no expectations about the nature of the job.

When recruiting youth workers, select people to meet specific needs, not simply to fill job vacancies. Here is a sample needs list for recruiting youth workers:

1. Senior high Sunday night counselors
2. Junior high Sunday night counselors
3. Bible study teachers
4. Sunday school teachers
5. Disciplers of females and males
6. Youth coordinators
7. Music leaders
8. Representatives to church boards
9. Media resource persons

As you list your program's needs, you will probably envision individuals in your church you might approach about becoming youth workers. With a precise list of job openings, you can ask a person to be responsible for a specific task.

To be up front about job expectations, write job descriptions for each need. This helps you and the prospective youth worker understand what is expected from the very beginning. Be sure the job description mentions the approximate amount of time each responsibility will require. Remember that you can be flexible and negotiate the job descriptions; if a person does not feel comfortable with a particular task, remove it. This is a guideline, not a law! Let it affirm the ministry of a youth worker.

Below are sample job descriptions I used at Trinity Hill. The first is for a person to help lead the teaching portion of our junior high Sunday night program (about twenty-five minutes each week). I helped this person gather resource materials for the time and gave some direction on content.

```
Trinity Hill United Methodist Church
Job Description
Name:
Position Title: Youth Counselor—Jr. High
Youth Fellowship Teacher
Description of responsibilities and time re-
quired:
1. Prepare and teach the weekly Sunday night
youth fellowship class weekly from 6:30 p.m.
to 8:00 p.m. (two and a half hours per week).
2. Meet with the youth minister and coun-
selors each Sunday from 5:45 p.m. to 6:30
p.m. for planning, coordinating and prayer
(forty-five minutes per week).
3. Be present at bi-monthly counselors' fel-
lowship for a period of interaction and
evaluation (three hours every other month).
4. When possible, be with youth at planned
activities to enhance relationships and
chaperon (no time estimate).
5. When possible, attend youth worker train-
ing workshops when they are made available
(no time estimate).
6. Be available to youth for counseling, ad-
vice or other needs (no time estimate).
7. Pray for the youth ministry at Trinity
Hill (no time estimate).
8. One hour plan (one hour per week):
a. Make three phone calls to three youth per
week.
b. Send three postcards to three youth per
week.
```

THE HEART OF YOUTH MINISTRY

In every youth group, certain time consuming things must be done: mailings, preparing food and arranging chaperons for trips, for example. The person who fills the following job description saves me about three hours per week.

Trinity Hill United Methodist Church
Job Description
Name:
Position Title: Youth Counselor—Coordinator/Facilitator
Description of responsibilities and time required:
1. Coordinate those who provide the weekly snack for the Sunday night youth programs to ensure maximum efficiency (one hour per week).
2. Meet with the youth minister and counselors each Sunday from 5:45 p.m. to 6:30 p.m. for planning, coordinating and prayer (forty-five minutes per week).
3. Be present at every Sunday night youth fellowship program from 6:30 p.m. to 8:00 p.m. to help coordinate the snack supper and to be available as a resource person for the youth teachers (one and a half hours per week).
4. Be present at a bi-monthly counselors' fellowship for a period of interaction and evaluation (three hours every other month).
5. When possible, be with youth at planned activities to enhance relationships and chaperon (no time estimate).
6. When possible, attend youth worker training workshops when they are made available (no time estimate).
7. Help coordinate youth activities with the youth minister (two hours per month).
8. Be available to the youth for counseling, advice or other needs (no time estimate).

9. Pray for the youth ministry at Trinity Hill (no time estimate).
10. One hour plan (one hour per week):
a. Make three phone calls to three youth per week.
b. Send three postcards to three youth per week.

In addition to using specific job descriptions, another good recruiting strategy is to use people of all kinds in your ministry. Our natural human tendency is to enlist people who are just like us. But make an effort to recruit people of different ages and stages of life. The person with a quiet demeanor can minister in ways that the boisterous person can never do. The divorcee can have real empathy with the youth whose parents are separated. You need moms and dads, young couples and grandparents to give your leadership team a solid, multi-faceted base.

Finally, your recruiting approach should include honestly discussing the spiritual lives of prospective youth workers. Very often, your encouragement will help their spiritual lives skyrocket. Find out where they are in their pilgrimages with God, but do not let this be the only measuring stick you use in determining whether they should join the ministry team. I remember vividly a youth counselor who walked up to me after a youth communion service with tears in his eyes. "Thank you for asking me to be a counselor," he said. "I have grown so much as a Christian because of working with the youth."

Teaching them the Ropes—Training a Ministry Team

My philosophy on training youth workers is very simple. I think O.J.T. (on-the-job training) is the best teacher. Once the concept of relational ministry is explained to and understood by the youth worker, and the job description is agreed upon, my advice is like Rocky's: "Go for it!" Give the new recruits some background information on the group (i.e., cliques, leaders, troublemakers, etc.). With some direction, the new youth worker will usually pitch in and do the job well.

This is not to say that some formal training is not helpful. For example, I teach our ministry team the principles explained in this book. The funnel ministry concept (see chapter four) is described so that everybody knows where we are headed. I encourage attendance and even have the church pay for ministry team members to attend training events sponsored by denominational leadership, parachurch ministries and youth ministry organizations. Youth Specialties events, Asbury Theological Seminary's Youth Ministry Institute, Frazer Memorial Church Growth Seminar and other groups offer training sessions that help the team stay motivated and fresh.

Another helpful practice is to share what you read with the ministry team. Good articles or books ought to be passed on, especially to those on the team with teaching responsibilities. Circulating quality resources can go a long way to equip the youth worker to better teach God's Word.

Try to meet with your team on a weekly or bi-weekly basis. At the Wilmore church, for example, Hule meets with his team every Tuesday for lunch from September through May. This helps youth workers deal with their frustrations, share what God is doing in their areas of ministry, plan upcoming events and pray for each other.

The Care and Feeding of a Ministry Team

The folks on your ministry team are people with real needs, too! They are a part of your responsibility as a youth leader. Be sure that you are sensitive to their spiritual and emotional needs. For example, if you see a counselor "dragging in" on Sunday morning and you find out he was gone all week on a business trip, tell him to stay home. Find another counselor to cover for him.

Try to remember special days like anniversaries or birthdays by buying a card or a sheet cake for the person. Find ways to let your ministry team members know they are appreciated and their contribution is vital. For example, whenever one of our counselors retires, we say goodbye in a special way by having him or her sit on a chair in the middle of the room while the youth and other counselors share what that person has meant to them.

Once a year, take the ministry team and their families out to eat at a restaurant. Tell them this is a small way of saying thank you for their ministry to the youth. We also try to get together at a counselor's home three or four times a year for an informal fellowship time. All these things help the team feel valued.

Do not forget your counselors' spiritual needs. Encourage them to participate in Sunday school, small groups and retreats. Take their spiritual pulse periodically. They need your ministry, too!

The "Four M" Approach to Youth Ministry

We use what we call a "Four M" approach to team ministry. First, the *model* for our team ministries is servanthood:

> *Jesus called them [his disciples] together and said, "You know that those who are regarded as rulers of the Gentiles lord it over them, and their high officials exercise authority over them. Not so with you. Instead, whoever wants to become great among you must be your servant, and whoever wants to be first must be slave of all. For even the Son of Man did not come to be served, but to serve, and to give his life as a ransom for many" (Mark 10:42-45).*

The *mission* for our team ministries is the Great Commission:

> *Then Jesus came to them and said, "All authority in heaven and on earth has been given to me. Therefore go and make disciples of all nations, baptizing them in the name of the Father and of the Son and of the Holy Spirit, and teaching them to obey everything I have commanded you. And surely I am with you always, to the very end of the age" (Matthew 28:18-20).*

The *motivation* for our team ministries is the Holy Spirit:

> *"But you will receive power when the Holy Spirit comes on you; and you will be my witnesses in Jerusalem, and in all Judea and Samaria, and to the ends of the earth" (Acts 1:8).*

The *message* for our team ministries is Jesus Christ, the Living Water:

> Jesus answered, "Everyone who drinks this water will be thirsty again, but whoever drinks the water I give him will never thirst. Indeed, the water I give him will become in him a spring of water welling up to eternal life" (John 4:13-14).

May our team ministries always reflect these four M's as we minister!

12 The Commission

Youth Can Make a Difference in the World

By Hule Goddard

In this book we have examined relational ministry and why it is necessary for success in meeting young people where they are and moving them to where God wants them to be. We have explored ways to make our programs and our relational ministry discipleship oriented. We have discussed methods of helping young people become more dedicated to God and to the principles of his Word so they can become servants/leaders who will make a difference in the world.

We have also seen how God desires the family and church's burden to be that people would come to God, grow in his ways, become disciple followers of Christ and serve the kingdom of God.

We have defined the essential components needed to build an effective youth ministry from the ground up. One is that the youth minister's own spiritual life be in tune and his or her family's needs assume their proper priority. Next, establish an effective program that includes come, grow, discipleship and leadership training level ministries. (We suggested some practical techniques and special events to do this.)

We considered the importance of the ministry team and focused on what I feel is the central theme of the Scriptures, as well as this book—relational ministry as the heart of youth ministry.

However, all the principles, Scriptures, philosophical and theological concepts, program techniques and practical techniques that could be amassed in hundreds of years are useless without that passion described in Jeremiah 20:9, "But if I say, 'I will not mention him [God] or speak any more in his name,' his word is in my heart like a fire, shut up in my bones. I am weary of holding it in; indeed, I cannot." We must be filled with the *agape* love that God has given us through the ministry of the Holy Spirit (Romans 5:5 says, "God has poured out his love into our hearts by the Holy Spirit. . ."), until, like young Jeremiah, we cannot help being consumed by a desire to reach out to God and other people. Until this happens, significant, vital youth ministry will not take place in our churches, regardless of our knowledge, our salaries or the time that we spend in ministry. However, passionate *agape* love, coupled with sound youth ministry principles and techniques, is a powerful mixture sure to be effective in meeting young people where they are and moving them toward God.

Jorge once befriended a young Roman Catholic girl during his ministry at Trinity Hill Church. As he spent time with her, and as Jorge's youth group began to welcome her, she agreed to attend a retreat involving ten churches from Ohio and Kentucky. At this retreat, the young girl witnessed God moving in a powerful way. Of the 250 young people who were there, 225 came forward to make a deeper commitment to God. During the week she watched people making commitments, sharing their brokenness, witnessing to one another and being reconciled to God and each other through repentance and confession.

On Sunday morning, the young people took turns standing and telling what the weekend had meant to them. When this young lady stood up, it was obvious that she had never testified before and that she was not accustomed to sharing in a big group. As she nervously, and with a red face, began to speak, it was one of the most profound moments of my ministry. She said with conviction, "Oh, you Methodists. You are so on fire. In my church, I have not seen this kind of life-changing fire." How many churches across our nation lack the "fire" of which she spoke?

It is my prayer that whatever the denomination, people

in every community around this country would say, "Oh, you youth workers. You people in youth ministry are so on fire that we have got to respond. Things have to happen." Indeed, I pray that God's fire will be so shut up in our bones that we will do whatever it takes to reach youth. When our hearts become one with God's heart, when we have that kind of determination, lives will change, youth ministry will be effective and young people will come to know the living God.

Now is the time to put the Great Commission into action: "go and make disciples of all nations, baptizing them in the name of the Father and of the Son and of the Holy Spirit, and teaching them to obey everything I have commanded you. And surely I will be with you always, to the very end of the age" (Matthew 28:19-20). This is our Lord's Commission. It is time for us to fulfill it in our churches and communities with a relational, discipleship-oriented approach that is the heart of youth ministry.

Bibliography

Becchetti, Noel, ed. *Youth Worker*, Summer 1984. El Cajon: Youth Specialties, 1985.

Bilhartz, Terry, D. *Francis Asbury's American.* Grand Rapids: Francis Asbury Press, 1984.

Dollen, Charles, J. *The Catholic Tradition.* U.S.A.: McGarth Publishing Co., 1979.

Foster, Richard, J. *Celebration of Discipline.* San Francisco: Harper and Row Publishers, 1978.

Irving, Roy, G., Ed. *Youth and the Church.* Chicago: Moody Press, 1974.

MacDonald, Gordon. *Ordering Your Private World.* Nashville: Thomas Nelson Inc., 1984.

Merton, Thomas. *The Wisdom of the Desert.* New York: New Directions Publishing Corp., 1960.

Nouwen, Henri, J.M. *Making All Things New.* San Francisco: Harper and Row, Publishers, 1981.

Parkhurst, Louis Gifford, Jr. *Answers to Prayer.* Minneapolis: Bethany House Publishers, 1983.

Park, Percy, Livingston, ed. *The Journal of John Wesley.* Chicago: Moody Press.

Reapsome, James W. *Youthletter.* Philadelphia: Evangelical Ministries, Inc., 1985.

Stevens, Doug. *Called to Care.* Grand Rapids: Zondervan Publishing House, 1985.

End Notes

Chapter 2

1. Les Christie, *Unsung Heroes* (Grand Rapids, Michigan: Zondervan Publishing House, 1987), p. 25.
2. The Gallup Report, *Religion in America,* reported by the Princeton Religion Research Center, Inc., March 1984, p. 67.
3. The Gallup Report, p. 71.
4. "A Nation of Step Families," *Youth Worker Update,* December 1986, p. 6.
5. "New Stats on Teen Sex," *Youth Worker Update,* February 1987, p. 5.
6. William H. Willimon & Robert L. Wilson, *Rekindling the Flame: Strategies for a Vital United Methodism,* (Nashville: Abingdon Press, 1987), p. 42.

Chapter 6

1. Tony Campolo, "Passionless Generation," *Youth Worker Update,* Summer 1985, pp. 16-21.

Chapter 7

1. Tony Campolo, "Passionless Generation," *Youth Worker Update,* Summer 1985, pp. 16-21.
2. Ibid.

Chapter 8

1. Gary Smalley and John Trent. *The Blessing.* Nashville: Thomas Nelson Publishers, 1986, p. 35.

Chapter 9

1. Dr. Steve Harper, "All along the way" (Wilmore: Holy Spirit in the Life of a Minister, 1985).
2. Gordon MacDonald, *Ordering Your Private World* (Nashville: Thomas Nelson Inc., 1984), p. 8.
3. Rev. Charles J. Dollen, *The Catholic Tradition*

(U.S.A.: McGarth Publishing Co., 1979), pp. 27-29.

4. Henri J.M. Nouwen, *The Way of the Heart* (New York: The Seminary Press, 1981), pp. 14-33.

5. Dollen, pp. 93-95.

6. Ibid, pp. 373-375.

7. Percy Livingstone Parker, ed., *The Journal of John Wesley* (Chicago: Moody Press), pp. 14-247.

8. Terry D. Bilhartz, *Francis Asbury's America* (Grand Rapids: Francis Asbury Press, 1984), pp. 9-125.

9. Louis Gifford Parkhurst Jr, *Answers to Prayer* (Minneapolis: Bethany House Publishers, 1983), pp. 44-46.

10. Thomas Merton, *The Wisdom of the Desert* (New York: New Directions Publishing Corp., 1960), pp. 3-20.

11. Nouwen, pp. 14-33.

12. Richard J. Foster, *Celebration of Discipline* (San Francisco: Harper and Row Publishers, 1978), pp. 13-63.

13. Foster, pp. 13-163.

14. Ibid., p. 1.

15. Ibid., p. 6

16. Ibid.

17. Noel Becchetti, "A Word From the Editor" *Youth Worker* (Summer 1984), p. 1.

18. Ibid., p. 1.

19. Mick Yconelli, "Ministering to High School Students," (Chicago: Lecture at National Youth Workers Convention, 1985).

20. Doug Stevens, *Called to Care* (Grand Rapids: Zondervan Publishing House, 1985), p. 53.

21. Ibid, p. 61

22. Ibid., p. 72

23. Ibid

24. MacDonald, p. 29.

25. Ibid., p. 12

26. Henri J.M. Nouwen, *Making All Things New* (San Francisco: Harper and Row Publishers, 1981), p. 69.

27. Nouwen, *The Way of the Heart*, p. 25.

28. Ibid., 36-37.

29. Foster, p. 34.

30. MacDonald.

Appendix

The following is a reprint of a handout used to recruit young people to the Leadership Training I—VI program at Tyler Street United Methodist Church in Dallas, Texas. Note that it provides an honest overview of what leadership training demands and offers.

Tyler Street Leadership Program

The world has gone crazy: starved for leadership, direction and purpose. Millions of people stumble along being distracted, destroyed by immorality, drugs, selfishness, hate, depression, boredom. They are crying out for hope, help and direction as they experience the narthex of hell.

Who is going to bring change? Who is going to help them? Who is going to radically turn our world back to the God who made them? God? He's done the ultimate already. He came in the person of Jesus to bring the solution to Adam's problem (selfishness).

Yet the purposes, the desires of God, will not be realized in human lives if you do not wholeheartedly give yourself to him and to the task of being world-changers. Who is going to bring the change? GOD, through YOU! No great or lasting change, revival, renewal or awakening has come to mankind without a godly leader.

I feel strongly that God has his hand on this youth group and from its youth, leaders—both men and women—will be raised up. Their lives will literally change the course of history, effect governments, win thousands to Jesus Christ, build solid churches, revive Methodism, the possibilities are limitless.

Training everyone who is willing to pay the price to see this vision realized is what Leadership I—VI is all about. If you desire to find your calling, your place in God's plan and give yourself wholeheartedly to it, then be sure to read, carefully, the following course descriptions and register for the appropriate leadership class.

Leadership I and II

From the beginning, when God wanted to move in this

world he chose to use men and women: to lead his people, speak his Word, accomplish his work. That is the root and heart of leadership. To open ourselves to God—to know him, his will, his ways, his plans, his works and to bring these to people. (Thus, we must relate to them, know them, love them, serve them, forgive them, call them, challenge them, teach them, encourage them and lead them to God.)

In the Bible we find the history of leaders God raised up and used to bring about his will on the earth—Abraham, Jacob, Joseph, Moses, Joshua, Caleb, Ruth, Samuel, Saul, David, Solomon, Esther, kings, prophets, Nehemiah, Jesus, (the perfect example/leader, God himself among us), Peter, Paul and Timothy. God continues to use leaders— Augustine, Martin Luther, John Wesley, you and me.

I. We begin each session of our Leadership Training Program with a short study of each of the people mentioned above—to learn from leadership characteristics and skills we can apply to our lives to make us better leaders.

II. We will then cover practical areas of becoming strong, consistent men and women of Christlike character. Emphasis will be given to obtaining consistent:

    A. quiet time—quality and quantity

    B. growing, victory over witness-destroying sin

    C. hate for sin, love for God and good

    D. Christian lifestyles

III. Study the essential components of effective leadership:

    A. character

    B. skill

    C. experience

IV. Assign responsibilities for actual leadership roles.

V. We will motivate ourselves to consistent commitment through systems of accountability.

Leadership III and IV

Effective leaders must be people who are led, grounded, balanced, safe-guarded and inspired by the Word of God. A hopscotch knowledge of biblical goodies is not sufficient for the person called to provide sound, practical, strong leadership on the job and in the church.

Thus, Leadership III and IV is designed to help you see the big picture of God's dealings with us from Genesis to Revelation. An emphasis on the major themes of the Bible will help disclose the things dearest to the heart of God, and study of the Bible as a whole will help you gain a sense of balance and perspective in which to place topical insights you have already obtained.

Of course, study without application is almost worthless. Thus, practical, daily application will be expected and emphasized. The classes will include:

I. In-class (one and a half hours weekly) presentation of major sections of Scripture, emphasizing content and meaning.

II. Follow-up by reading the Scripture just presented and completing a "project sheet" on the lesson (to be done outside class) emphasizing application.

III. Reviewing the "project sheets" for last week's lesson at the beginning of class. Sharing applications or clearing up any questions.

IV. Monthly meeting with youth pastor to share progress, insights and commitments.

Leadership V and VI

Having understood leadership, striving and attaining at least a degree of consistency, discovering your unique gifts, talents and abilities, then tempering and coaching this with the Word of God, you are ready to begin your ministry within our youth group.

The following ministries are offered this fall and spring for those qualified and called to them.

1. Teaching seventh and eighth grade Bible studies (six teachers needed).
2. Evangelism Captains—(Love of Christ course prerequisite).
3. Director of Big Brother/Big Sister Ministry.
4. Discipling Ministry.
5. Administrative Ministry in Youth Office.
6. Creative Helps Director.
7. Hot-Line-For-Help Director.
8. Go-For-The-Gold Director.
9. Peacemaking, trouble-shooting, mercy, ministry.
10. Missions Ministry.
11. Others unique to your gifts—our needs.

Also, once you have chosen your ministry you should:
1. Coordinate all activities with youth office.
2. Attend bi-monthly prayer and share times—Tuesdays, 6:30 a.m.